Thanks
We would like to thank all the athletes, coaches and
family members who contributed their stories for this
play. We would also like to thank Northumbria University
and Matthew Jones.

Presented by Murmur and Live Theatre

THE PRIZE

Steve Gilroy and Richard Stockwell

First presented at Live Theatre
Wednesday 25 July to Saturday 28 July 2012

Underbelly, Edinburgh
Wednesday 1 August to Sunday 26 August 2012

Live Theatre
Wednesday 29 August to Saturday 8 September 2012

The Prize is one of the outstanding projects granted the
London 2012 Inspire Mark, the badge of the London
2012 Inspire Programme, which recognises exceptional
and innovative projects inspired by the 2012 Games.

THE PRIZE

Steve Gilroy and Richard Stockwell

CAST
Chris Connel
Seroca Davis
Helen Embleton
Melissa Johns
Carl Kennedy

CREATIVE TEAM

Director	**Steve Gilroy**
Assistant Director	**Rosie Kellagher**
Designer	**Gary McCann**
Production Manager/Lighting Designer	**Drummond Orr**
Composer	**Jeremy Bradfield**
AV Designer	**James McAleer**
Movement Direction	**Rachel Krische**
Stage Manager	**Paul Aziz**
ASM	**James Piercy**

CAST

Chris Connel
Characters include: *Norman Strike, Richard Cobbing*

His theatre credits include: *Close the Coalhouse Door* (Northern Stage/Live Theatre), *The Pitmen Painters* (Live Theatre, National Theatre and Broadway), *Nativities,* Stuart in the premiere of *Cooking With Elvis, Toast* (Live Theatre), *Shooting the Legend* (Theatre Royal Newcastle), *Cooking With Elvis, Bouncers, Studs, Up on Roof, A Kick in the Baubles* (Hull Truck), *Bouncers,* (Ambassadors Theatre and tour), *Black on White Shorts* (Paines Plough/Live Theatre), *And a Nightingale Sang* (Cheltenham Everyman), *The Steal, Men Women Inspectors and Dogs* (Theatre Royal York/Cloud Nine), *Peer Gynt* (Three Over Eden Theatre Company). Film credits include: *Goal* and *Purely Belter.* Television credits include: *Emmerdale* (YTV), *The Round Tower* (Festival Films), *Badger* (BBC/Feelgood Fiction), *The Bill* (ITV), *Byker Grove* (BBC/Zenith), *Quayside* (Zenith/Tyne Tees), *King Leek* (Granada Television), *Heartbeat* (YTV), *Crocodile Shoes* (series 1 and 2); (BBC), *How We Used to Live* (YTV), *Finney* (Zenith/Carlton), *The Block* (Channel 4), *Take Me* (Scottish TV/Coastal Productions), *Breeze Block* (BBC), *Steel River Blues* (Granada), *Lawless* (Company/ITV), *George Gently* (Company/BBC) and *Navy of the Damned.* Radio work includes: *The Gallery, The Pitmen Painters, Poor Clare, The Song Thief, A Man's World* and *Skellig* (BBC Radio Drama).

Seroca Davis
Characters include: *Anne Wafula Strike, Hilary Hardy*

Her theatre credits include: *Little Baby Jesus* (Oval House), *Random* (Royal Court Theatre), *Love's Labour's Lost* (Shakespeare's Globe and USA Tour), *We the People* (Shakespeare's Globe), *Don Juan In Soho* (Donmar Warehouse), *Master Juba* (Albany), *93.2fm* (Royal Court Theatre), *Little Sweet Thing* (UK Theatre Tour).
TV includes: *Doctor Who, Criminal Justice, Horne and Corden, That Mitchell and Webb Look, Prime Suspect, The Bill, Snap, Homework High, Daylight Robbery II, Holby City.* Her film work includes: *London Birds Can't Fly, Kidscape* and *Innocent Pink.*

Helen Embleton

Characters include: *Viv Mills, Rachel Gamble-Flint*

Her theatre credits include: *Next Swan Down the River Might be Black* (Tara Arts), *Oh! What A Lovely War* (Northern Stage), *Sleeping Beauty, The Tempest* (Customs House), *Stand N Tan* (Open Clasp), *Cinderella* (Durham Gala), *Motherland* (Live Theatre/ Empty Space – Winner of The Stage Best Ensemble), *Pub Quiz* (New Writing North) and *Iron* (Live Theatre – Winner of the Spotlight Award Best Actress). Her film work includes: *Context* (Dandy Lion) and *Perfect Ten* (Independent). Radio credits include: *Concrete Jungle* (BBC), *Bath Time* (New Writing North), *Belsay Poem* (Picture House Exhibition) and *Saturday Matinee* (Tyneside Cinema).

Melissa Johns

Characters include: *Jess Eddie, Beth Davidson, Kat Copeland*

Melissa has recently graduated from East 15 Acting School. Winning the Laurence Olivier Bursary Award (2011), she also enjoyed many successes such as a devised show *Doing the Idiots*, directed by Alexander Zeldin, in which she performed at the National Theatre Studio and *INK* directed by Andrea Ling which had a successful run at the Edinburgh Fringe 2011. Melissa is very excited to be working with Live Theatre and Murmur.

Carl Kennedy

Characters include: *Roger Black, Nick Beighton, Ali Jawad*

Carl trained at Manchester Metropolitan University and after graduating moved to the North East (Newcastle) where he now lives and works as an actor for theatre, television and film. He has worked on productions for Live Theatre (Newcastle), Northern Stage (Newcastle), The Globe Theatre, Bristol Old Vic and many more. Carl is an experienced improviser with the Improvisation Foundation and its award-winning comedy improv company The Suggestibles.

CREATIVE TEAM

Paul Aziz
Stage Manager

Paul has worked in theatre since 1993 when he began as a stage technician and has since worked in many productions as a freelance stage manager as well as taking on the roles of Production/Company/Stage Manager. Paul's first production for Live Theatre as a Stage Manager was in *When We Were Queens* (2002). His other credits include: *Top Girls* (2006), *Things of Dry Hours* (2007), *The Pitmen Painters* (2008), *A Northern Odyssey* (2010) and *A Walk On Part* (2011).

Jeremy Bradfield
Composer

Jeremy Bradfield is a composer, sound designer and multi-instrumental performer. He completed his Masters in Music at Newcastle University in 2009 after being presented the Sager Foundation Award for composition, a scholarship funded by Sting. Since May 2010, Jeremy has worked as a Project Musician at the Sage Gateshead and regularly performs as a percussionist with the Newcastle Flamenco Collective. Theatre includes: *Attempts On Her Life* (Northumbria University), *Playing The Building* (The Sage Gateshead), *La Chanson du Retour* (Théâtre Sans Frontières/The Sage Gateshead), *Where Those That Stood Before* (FallenFromGrace). Future productions include sound design for *Blue Boy*, a new play by Margaret Wilkinson in partnership with Northern Stage.

Steve Gilroy
Writer/Director

As writer/director, Steve's credits include: *Facts on the Ground* (Live Theatre), *Hand Me Down* (The Pleasance/Romanian International Theatre Festival/Live Theatre), *Motherland* (UK Tour/Live Theatre/Underbelly), *Naturalised* (Royal Court Theatre, Young Writers Festival), *Now We're Ten* (Yvonne Arnaud Studio Theatre). As director, credits include: *Lion* (Live Theatre), *Mine* (Live Theatre), *Reality* (Royal Shakespeare Company/Live Theatre), *Lazarus* (Gala Theatre, Durham), *Me and Cilla* (Live Theatre), *Iron* (Northern Stage), *Home by Now* (Baltic), *Top Girls* (Live Theatre), *Ballroom Cougars* (Live Theatre/New Writing North), *The Censor* (UCT Studio Theatre, Cape Town S.A.), *Terrorism* (Oval House), *In the Family, Mr*

Sinclair's Teeth, Trace (Royal Court), *Ultra Violet* (Royal Court/ Duke of York's Theatre), *Act Without Words* (Embassy Theatre, Central School of Speech and Drama), *TV Tots Meet Bomb Boy* (London New Plays Festival, Riverside Studios), *Life On Mars* (Riverside Studios) and *Coming Out* (Liverpool Everyman).

Awards: Scotsman Fringe First, The Stage Best Ensemble Award, The Jack Tinker Spirit of The Fringe Award (*Motherland*), Nomination Fringe First (*Hand Me Down*).

Rosie Kellagher
Assistant Director

Rosie has worked as a director and assistant director with theatre companies including Soho Theatre, The Arches, Vanishing Point and the Royal Lyceum. She was Associate Producer at Glasgow's *A Play, A Pie And A Pint* for which she also directed many productions. Her production of *Tir Nan Og* at the Assembly Rooms won Best New Musical at the 2007 Edinburgh Festival Fringe and she also won the 2007 Arches Award for Stage Directors.

Rachel Krische
Movement Direction

Rachel is a member of an innovative Performing Arts Department at Leeds Metropolitan University where she is Course Leader and Senior Lecturer in Dance. Before moving to Yorkshire, she spent 20 years as a London-based independent dance artist, collaborating and performing with over 20 different choreographers including: La Ribot, Akram Khan, Deborah Hay and Wendy Houstoun. She has been rehearsal director for several British dance companies, choreographed her own work and taught extensively. In 2002 she won the Jerwood Choreography Award with Ben Wright. Alongside her pedagogic practice Rachel maintains her profile as a practising artist, most recently touring her solo *The Swimmer* to several prestigious international festivals. She is currently working with Matthias Sperling, touring the duet *Do Not Be Afraid* and with Oliver Bray, touring the duet *Ryan*.

James McAleer
AV Designer

James McAleer is a cinematographer whose credits range from international commercials, feature films, and award-winning shorts through to prime time and live television. He has just completed principal photography on the feature film *Harrigan* starring Stephen Tompkinson, a period police drama set during the miners' strike and blackouts of 1974. James' own experimental film *Invertebrate* was long-listed for the 2012 BAFTA award in the short film category.

Gary McCann
Designer

Originally from County Armagh, Northern Ireland, Gary trained at Nottingham Trent University. Now based in Greenwich, London, he has achieved international recognition as a designer for theatre and opera.

Current and future projects include: *Die Fledermaus* (Norwegian National Opera), *The Flying Dutchman* (Ykaterinburg Opera, Russia), *Aida and the Barber of Seville* (Nationale Reisopera, Holland), *Owen Wingrave* (Opera Trionfo Amsterdam) and *The Odd Couple* (Perth Theatre).

His recent design work includes *The Pitmen Painters* which was produced at the Duchess Theatre in the West End following runs at Live Theatre, the National Theatre (Cottesloe and Lyttelton spaces), The Friedman Theatre on Broadway, the Volkstheater in Vienna, and two national tours – the production won the Best New Play award at the Evening Standard Awards in 2009. *Three Days in May* has recently finished a West End run following a UK tour – the play was winner of the What's On Stage Best New Play Award in 2012 and is due for revival later this year. In summer 2012 *A Walk-On Part* completed a West End season at the Arts Theatre following two runs at the Soho Theatre.

Other recent work includes: *33 Variations* (Volkstheater, Vienna), *La Voix Humaine*, *L'Heure Espagnole* (Nationale Reisopera), *The Girl in the Yellow Dress* (Market Theatre, Johannesburg, Stadttheater Stockholm, nominated for Best Set Design at the South African Naledi Awards), *Guys and Dolls* (Theater Bielefeld, Germany), *La Pietra del Paragone* (Opera Trionfo, Amsterdam), *Someone Who'll Watch Over Me*, *Moonlight and Magnolias* (Perth

Theatre), *Fidelio* (Garsington Opera, revival happening in 2014), *Norma* (National Opera of Moldova), *Così Fan Tutte* (Royal Academy of Music) and *Così Fan Tutte* (Schönbrunn Palace, Vienna).

His work has been exhibited at the V&A museum in London twice – as part of the *Collaborators* and *Transformation/ Revelation* exhibitions.

He is a member of Ransom Collective in Belfast.

Drummond Orr
Production Manager & Lighting Designer

Drummond has over thirty years' experience as a theatre electrician and stagehand, lighting designer and production manager. In that time he has toured nationally and internationally. He has worked in both touring and production theatre including: The RSC, Scottish Opera Theatre Royal - Newcastle, The Gulbenkian Studio, Opera North, Vincent Dance, Told By An Idiot, Northern Stage, Merce Cunningham Dance Company, Monster Productions and Theatre Royal – Drury Lane. In 2004 he took a 'short term' contract with Live Theatre to production manage their spring season. He is still searching for the exit. After fifteen years of almost continual touring Drummond put his bag on top of the wardrobe and spent five years teaching Technical Theatre skills, Stage Management and Stagecraft at National Diploma, HND and Degree levels.

Richard Stockwell
Writer

Richard began writing for commercial theatre; his thriller *Killing Time* went on a number one tour in 1998 and has since been produced fifteen times in nine countries and six languages – with the most recent productions earlier this year in India and Poland – as well as having been filmed in the US. *Future Shock* played at the Manchester 24:7 Festival 2011 and is winner of the Drama Association of Wales Best One-Act play of 2011. Other plays include: *Bad Blood* (UK Tour), *Trust and Madness* (Pomegranate Theatre Chesterfield), *Pinocchio* for which he wrote book and lyrics (Gordon Craig Theatre, Stevenage). Television: Richard wrote for *EastEnders* for two years as well as being commissioned to write *Death by Drowning*, an Agatha Christie story for the BBC.

ABOUT MURMUR

Murmur is a new theatre company which comprises experienced practitioners who are committed to producing new work of high quality in the North East of England. The company seeks to develop collaborations between artists from a range of disciplines in order to develop original theatre practice. This production is a step towards establishing Murmur as a leading and innovative new writing company working in the region.

ABOUT LIVE THEATRE

From its base on Newcastle's quayside, Live Theatre produces work as varied and diverse as the audiences it engages with. To do this it:

- Creates and performs new plays of world-class quality

- Finds and develops creative talent

- Unlocks the potential of young people through theatre

Founded in 1973, the theatre was recently transformed via a £5.5 million redevelopment. The result is a beautifully restored and refurbished complex of five Grade II listed buildings with state-of-the-art facilities in a unique historical setting, including a 160-seat cabaret style theatre, a studio theatre, renovated rehearsal rooms, a series of dedicated writer's rooms as well as a thriving café, bar and pub.

In 2013 Live Theatre will have been creating plays on Tyneside for 40 years, look out for news of our celebrations in our anniversary year.

Supported by
ARTS COUNCIL ENGLAND

AT LIVE THEATRE

Chief Executive
Jim Beirne MBE

Artistic Director
Max Roberts

Operations Director
Wendy Barnfather

Administrator – Directors
Clare Overton

Literary Manager
Gez Casey

Literary Officer
Rosie Kellagher

**Associate Director
– Literary Department**
Steve Gilroy

**Administrator – Literary
Department**
Degna Stone

Production Manager
Drummond Orr

Technical Manager
Dave Flynn

Senior Technician
Mark Tolan

Finance Officer
Catherine Moody

Marketing Manager (Maternity Leave)
Claire Cockroft

Marketing Manager (Maternity Cover)
Cait Read

Marketing & Press Officer
Emma Hall

Marketing & Press Officer
Amy Corbett

Marketing & Press Assistant
Melanie Rashbrooke

Development Manager
Gillian Firth

**Associate Director – Education
& Participation**
Paul James

Drama Worker
Rachel Glover

Drama Worker
Phil Hoffmann

**Administrator – Education
& Participation**
Sam Bell

House Manager
Carole Wears

Deputy House Manager
Michael Davies

Duty Manager
Holly Sykes

Duty Manager
Ben Young

Administrator – Events & Hires
Nicole Huddart

**Stage Management & Duty
Technicians**
Paul Aziz, Heather Robertson

Frontline Staff
Rosa Aers, Amy Berry, Nina Berry,
Camille Burridge, Katie Dent,
Chris Foley, Niamh Lightfoot,
Caroline Liversidge,
Emily Merrit, Mark Gerrens,
Matthew Greenhough,
Helen Tuffnell, Charlotte
Wainwright, Emily Wray

THE PRIZE

Steve Gilroy & Richard Stockwell

THE PRIZE

OBERON BOOKS
LONDON

WWW.OBERONBOOKS.COM

First published in 2012 by Oberon Books Ltd.

521 Caledonian Road, London N7 9RH

Tel: +44 (0) 20 7607 3637 / Fax: +44 (0) 20 7607 3629

e-mail: info@oberonbooks.com

www.oberonbooks.com

Copyright © Steve Gilroy & Richard Stockwell, 2012

Steve Gilroy & Richard Stockwell are hereby identified as authors of this play in accordance with section 77 of the Copyright, Designs and Patents Act 1988. The authors have asserted their moral rights.

All rights whatsoever in this play are strictly reserved and application for performance etc. should be made before commencement of rehearsal to Independent Talent Group Ltd. Oxford House, 76 Oxford Street, London W1D 1BS. No performance may be given unless a licence has been obtained, and no alterations may be made in the title or the text of the play without the authors' prior written consent.

You may not copy, store, distribute, transmit, reproduce or otherwise make available this publication (or any part of it) in any form, or binding or by any means (print, electronic, digital, optical, mechanical, photocopying, recording or otherwise), without the prior written permission of the publisher. Any person who does any unauthorized act in relation to this publication may be liable to criminal prosecution and civil claims for damages.

A catalogue record for this book is available from the British Library.

PB ISBN: 978-1-84943-439-3

Digital ISBN: 978-1-84943-527-7

Printed, bound and converted
by CPI Group (UK) Ltd, Croydon, CR0 4YY.

Visit www.oberonbooks.com to read more about all our books and to buy them. You will also find features, author interviews and news of any author events, and you can sign up for e-newsletters so that you're always first to hear about our new releases.

Characters

CHARMIAN RAWLINGS (NÉE WELSH)
(A woman in her seventies from County Durham)

ROGER BLACK
(A man in his forties from Gosport)

JESS EDDIE
(A woman in her twenties from County Durham)

VIV MILLS
(A woman in her fifties from Coventry)

KIRA ROBERTS
(A woman in her twenties from London)

JOHN MAYOCK
(A man in his forties from Yorkshire)

BETH DAVIDSON
(A woman in her thirties from Darlington)

NICK GILLINGHAM
(A man in his forties from Walsall)

KAT COPELAND
(A woman in her twenties from Teesside)

ALI JAWAD
(A man in his twenties from Lebanon now London)

ANNE WAFULA STRIKE
(A woman in her forties from Kenya now Harlow)

NORMAN STRIKE
(A man in his sixties from South Shields now Harlow)

GERI BUCKLEY
(A woman in her twenties from Yorkshire)

SIMON WILSON
(A man in his fifties from Nottinghamshire

JAMES MCLEAN
(A man in his twenties from Southend)

RACHEL GAMBLE-FLINT
(A woman in her twenties from Darlington)

ALYSON DIXON
(A woman in her thirties from Sunderland)

FREYA MURRAY
(A woman in her twenties from Edinburgh now Newcastle)

WILL HARDY
(A boy aged fourteen from Newcastle)

HILARY HARDY
(A woman in her forties from Newcastle)

TIMMY STRIKE
(A boy aged nine from Harlow)

STEPHEN MILLER
(A man in his thirties from Newcastle)

RICHARD COBBING
(A man in his forties from Gateshead now London)

NICK BEIGHTON
(A man in his thirties from Shrewsbury)

NOTES:

Words in square brackets [ ] are not spoken but are for clarification of meaning.

A stroke (/) indicates the point of interruption.

A character's Line placed within the text of another indicates that the latter continues uninterrupted, therefore the characters are speaking simultaneously. For example:

HILARY: Well, yeah that's not fair, I suppose, in that you would wear them all day, [WILL: Yes, I would] Yeah, you'd wear them all day wouldn't you? Sorry that's wrong.

This text went to press before the end of rehearsals and some text may appear different to the performance.

SCENE 1

CHARMIAN is raised above the stage, as though on a high diving board. An image of black water is projected.

CHARMIAN: Ooooh yes. On the ten metre board, you could look south and see Redcar, you could look north and see, Sunderland. I've dived from the ten metre in a howling gale, rain, snow all sorts of weather I've done. Dawdon Pit Pond, yes. It was, water was always warm, always lovely and warm because it was the, the, it was the pit cooling pond so. Er, I understand that the water went round the engines, for the mining machinery, to cool them down and came in back all warm, there was a big pipe at the far end where the water tumbled out, lovely and warm, used to go and sit under the water there.

But er, ma, ma and I, we lived in Thornley and we used to take the bus down to Seaham. Then take the bus down into Dawdon and walk the last half mile or so to the pit. One thing that er, I, used to worry me a little, er is, when it was really windy and going off into a dive from ten metres, er would it make me go over or shah…or flat, would I hurt myself? But the wind never did, it made me turn but it never made me change my angle.

It was concrete on the bottom of the pool but then there was the kind of sludge, er which if it [was] undisturbed would probably be about this deep, you could go down there and bring up er, fistfuls of stuff and it was black, black, black you know but er…

And it's a sense, it's a sense of balance. It's a sense of balance but it's also being very aware of where you are in space. I used to do two and a half somersaults inward from ten metres. Now in Dawdon the water was dark and the sky was light, when I went to Blackpool for a, it was a, it was a, it was in Blackpool, can't remember it, championship? No, I don't think it was a championship, I think it was a…a trial again, erm, the ceiling was dark and the water was light, and I lost my sense of position and I

19

crashed. I, I landed, I did three somersaults and landed on the water curled up and I had two black eyes, the water came up into my eyes. I, I, I'd got the light and the dark mixed up. I dived again and this time I spun too slowly and I ended up with two long bruises down each thigh and actually the skin broken on my hip bone *(Claps hands.).* And there were times years later even now when I begin to sweat, my hands begin to sweat when I think about it because I still remember.

Fear. Fear of crashing again, it's not fun, water's awful hard yeah.

SCENE 2

ROGER BLACK enters and addresses the audience as a motivational speaker. A PowerPoint presentation in the background.

ROGER: Well, my opening gambit is, you make people laugh but I mean it's to get people…no, the opening gambit is to get people to buy in so y'know, my opening thing is, well I do a few gags to begin with but, that ultimately I'm here to share with you things that I learned throughout my career… Oh you'd like it from a theatre point of view, 'cause it's theatre. Yeah, 'cause what we do is, is, we open up the people's minds… I'm here to share with you things that I learned throughout my career that allowed me to not only run fast but to have my greatest day at the end of my career at the '96 Olympic games in Atlanta, where I won the Olympic medal, silver medal in the 400m. And then I say, the reason it's my greatest day is because it took place on the greatest stage of them all.

SLIDE PROJECTED.

Slide text 'Roger Black. 400m Runner. Silver medallist, Atlanta 1996.'

I'll give you a brochure so you can have an idea of it and then you're more than welcome to come and watch us because it, as you know, it's not what you talk about and what you do on paper, it's what you do in front of…the skill is, the, is the, is the, is the…is the delivery of it, and believing it, which I do.

Doesn't matter to you how fast I ran. It means nothing to you how fast I ran. If I told you I ran 44.1 or 44.6 it would make no difference to you at all. The medal is the medal. It's not defined by a time and that's it. So my overriding emotion was relief and then completion. This should never…this could easily not have happened because of all the injury and setbacks and they can nev – , this can never be taken away from me and that's it, y'know, and I will be defined by this moment for most of my life – which is true.

Let's dig deeper. So what does finding your passion mean? How we gunna do that? What does, y'know, belief, what does that mean to you? I mean, come on you're not going to run 44 seconds is it, it's not…but what does it mean to you?

SCENE 3

SLIDE PROJECTED.

Slide text 'Jessica Eddie. Rowing eight. Beijing 2008, fifth place. Selected for London 2012.'

JESS: I think I always wanted to. I knew from a very young age that I wanted to go to the Olympics. I really think. I think this year, and I've seen it so much more as it's turned into 2012, that the nation is taking pride in itself, and it is, it is getting more excited about, people, the world are going to be looking at us. This is the moment. And I think people are taking, and maybe it's the Jubilee as well, people are taking massive pride in Great Britain… I know it's costing a lot of money… I'm sorry about that…but… *(Laughing.)* that's the, that's the nature of the beast. It's…it's not the greatest show on earth for free.

CHORUS OF VOICES OVERLAPPING – Individual names appear and dissolve on the screen.

ROGER: I needed it. Because I didn't want to look back over my career and know that I'll have been given the chance and I didn't take it. I didn't want / to say if only.

JOHN: I've trained for fifteen years to get to the Olympic Games since I was ten, eleven years old... I've got one / chance. This might be my only chance.

JESS: Well, we, we qualified our boat last year at the world championships, so uhm, we came in the top five in the World Championships, earned a place, a berth, at the Olympics. Uhm...so we qualified. It was great.

VIV: Oh, the Olympics is everything. Before? My ambition was to learn to walk again.

JESS: So uhm...I pretty much, almost sealed my fate with, in that race in getting in. But I mean I've had to perform since then, and I've shown through my training that I'm still one of the top girls to be in the boat, so. / Yeah...

KIRA: ...it was always a goal to make an Olympics it doesn't have to be 2012, people are like all the time 'are you going to 2012, isn't your aim 2012?'

JESS: When it goes right, that's what makes it amazing. That you can get nine people on one day, for six minutes, thinking the same thing at the same time. Every stroke... Ahh.

Laughs.

JOHN: I had a few signals for me mum. I'd wink to me mum and I've kept that going / ever since.

KIRA: [The] hysteria with 2012 has been insane there are so many people who beforehand, had no Olympic / ambition...

JOHN: Erm, where I said to me mum and dad that on the start line I'd stroke me hair and also give them a wink to say hi, and also I'd give a wave / as well.

KIRA: ...and they all believe they can make it if they pour enough money into it and stuff, and I'm sure that's the case with a lot of sports to be honest. There's so much pressure from the / government...

BETH: Anyone wants to be an elite athlete you've got this 10,000 hours before you become an elite / performer...

JESS: I can. I've got a bit of a fiery temper. And, I know times that I've shouted in the boat when I shouldn't / have.

NICK: I had this burning, y'know, desire, this hunger for success, I hungered to achieve. Um ah, y'know it was deep inside of me... I don't settle for second best.

JESS: And then we started rowing like idiots. So we finished and I was... I was, I was trying my best not to like, let the frustration out. But uhm. We were looking at some pictures yesterday and I didn't look, happy. On the podium. I had a face like... I literally looked like I was sucking on a wasp.

Laughs.

JESS: Nothing has really lasted a terribly long time. And so, and to be honest it doesn't ree...it's, it's not something that I'm, that massively bothers me right now. Maybe the Olympics is, is my relationship.

JOHN: ...training twice a day, every day, giving up so much of your life when all your mates have been going to the pub and girlfriends and nightclubs and you've done none of that, you know?

KAT: It does worry me, what like, because, like what I'm going to do how I'm going to get a normal job how, I'm going to get a normal job when I finish.

JESS: I guess we've got really high expectations, every boat class. And I'd be gutted if we didn't win a medal. I think I'd be absolutely gu...yeah.

KIRA: 2012, can in no way live up to the expectations that everybody's putting on to it...

ALI: It was, for the last seven years it's been everything and unfortunately, you know, it hasn't gone my way but errr I have to be there somehow.

KIRA: I mean I'm sure you've heard all this stuff about how rubbish the logo is and like how like if you look at it then it looks like Lisa Simpson giving a blowjob…

KAT: I don't know exactly, there is like a motto isn't there, I mean I don't know what that is / but…

KIRA: …and like how like the opening ceremony is going to be in no way amazing as China's – all this stupid, stupid hype.

JESS: The thing is, I was in Beijing, and London is not gonna be Beijing. We're not gonna be like Beijing. London is not going to be like Beijing. They had endless, do you think, do you think the Chinese people were given a chance to look at the budgets for Beijing? I don't think so. So, yes, it's costing us nine billion pounds but I bet Beijing probably cost double that. I think there'll be a lot of cheery British people there and waving their Union Jacks and, joining in, and…and that's what we've got to offer you know. I don't need to see ten thousand drummers drumming in time 'cause I'm gonna see a morris dancer having a jig.

SCENE 4

ANNE and NORMAN are situated away from each other on either side of the stage.

ANNE: Yeh, where I grew up. I, I was born in Kenya, west erm part of Kenya, in a small town called erm Webuye and erm…

This erm, I mean in this very, very small village called Mihuu. It was that, very small. I was born as a normal, healthy child and when I was about two-and-a-half years I was struck down by polio. This was a surprise to the villagers because they knew of children who are born with a disability but they just did not understand how a healthy young girl, you know, a toddler would be running around one minute and the second minute she can't stand. She can't even talk, she can't even open her eyes. You know, she's lifeless. They did not understand that. They actually thought I'd been bewitched and some, because I was healthy, and then suddenly I couldn't walk, I couldn't, you know, I was actually half paralysed. They were so afraid of the curse going around the village and, but...it's just because, you know, lack of knowledge. They wanted me dead and if my parents could not give me up so that I could die then my parents were also not allowed to stay in the village.

NORMAN: Erm, we used to live in a bombed out area of Tyne Dock, when I was very small erm, called Lawson, corner of Lawson and Adelaide Street. Erm, and it was a very poor area, up and down houses, you know, outside toilets, that kind of thing. Hard upbringing in many ways, even though me dad worked, things weren't, you know, and when you leave school with no qualifications your options are very limited to what you can do with your hands really, and to a lesser extent your brain.

ANNE: Erm, I can remember, when I was still very young, crawling on my, you know, just crawling, wanting to play with my friends, my brothers and sisters and the stigma attached to it. They did not understand was what I had, was it contagious? ...they actually did not want their children to play with me.

NORMAN: Teachers. Teachers were just tyrants, they just used to cane ya...there was like nothing. It was all forced, they forced things into you in education. It was forced out of ya.

ANNE: Yeh, I am not a very good storyteller, yeh. I remember when I first went to school, erm, they took me to a school for the physically handicapped. The school is called Joyland which is in the south, Nianza, it was about two to three hours from the village where I was born...

NORMAN: I was a milkman for a while delivering bottles of milk. But that's, you had to get up too early in the bloody morning for that and it's freezing in the winter, so I didn't like that one at all.

ANNE: And... I remember the first time I went to school, I'm not a good storyteller. And Joyland was a boarding school, we had to be in school for three months and then we went home for one month and then we came back for another three months. So we only used to see our parents say three, three months in a year.

NORMAN: Erm, and then the steel works in Jarrow. And that was good coz I got a chance to do different kinds of jobs, coz I was a Crane Driver, an Overhead Crane Driver, trained me to do that. I quite enjoyed that until I knocked something into a pit and caused a load of damage and I was chucked off the cranes.

ANNE: This was a place where I felt normal, you know, I didn't feel like there was anything wrong with me because we were all disabled and I think that sometimes we would look around and there were other young people who were more severely disabled than I was and I sometimes would help feed them or you try to p... you know, try to dress them. But that really instilled a little bit of erm, some sense of erm, acceptance and love and feeling that actually I am normal human being.

NORMAN: [I] became what's called a button lad so where one conveyor belt transferred onto another conveyor belt you were there to make sure nothing got stuck in the shoot where the coal...coz sometimes great big lumps of coal or stone would come along, you'd have to stop it, unblock it, that kind of thing, really boring. I used to read about five books a week when I was doing that. Put a little light on and read. Err and then once I fell asleep and a big lump of stone got caught in the belt and of course I was asleep and I didn't notice and all the coal backed up and the belt snapped and the whole tunnel was blocked off. I got into real trouble, I almost got sacked over that one.

ANNE: …and it's my mam who used to come visit me and she would take me to school and come and get me from school. And I remember one of the, the teachers came and said 'Oh Olympia,' Olympia is actually my middle name, she said 'Oh Olympia, you are going home.' And I packed my suitcase and went to the office and I saw my eldest sister and I was, you know, I just sensed something wasn't right. I was about nine. I saw my eldest sister and you know, the first thing I said to her, I said 'Alice you're not supposed to be here, you're supposed to be in school.' And she said, 'Oh I know, mam just asked me to come and pick you up, you are supposed…we need you at home.'

NORMAN: Anything I could get me hands on err initially. Anything…errr…crime novels. Err, but then I'd always read books since I was a kid so I read Dickens… Jane Austen, Dostoyevsky. Blokes down the pit and I'd be sitting in the little train with me helmet on reading me book at four in the morning and they'd say what you reading, is it dirty book is it? And I'd say no it's Jane Austen actually. 'Jane wee? What does she write then? Is there sex in it?' 'Well no, you know it's a classic novel!' 'Alright, oh. Well, it must be bloody boring then.' You can imagine can't ya? So they always thought I was a bit eccentric. But I loved reading books, I always have done, all me life. Even though I came out without an education.

ANNE: And I kept insisting, 'Is something wrong, you know, has something happened?' I mean we sort of, you never just went home to visit unless, someone had died, you know? And we went, after we went home and my mam had, my mam had died, erm… So that happened erm, and I think when my mother died everything just changed. I started looking at life, you know, with a different eye because my mother was everything, she's, she, she meant everything to me. She bathed me, she looked after me, you know, she understood what was, because of my disability, and had been taken away just changed how I looked at life. Erm, she just collapsed you know but according…this, this is another mystery, according to the villagers she, she was bewitched. But to me I always think that maybe she had, maybe she had a heart attack or something like that.

NORMAN: It pre-dated the mine, I suppose. I'd sort of always been a kind of rebellious kind of person… Well, why's he the boss coz he's stupid. You know, that kind of thing. I had this err, this old man down the pit called Jimmy Scarth and he said to me 'Here read this.' And it was *The Communist Manifesto* I remember. And I took it away and I was trying to read it and it was all about dialectical? Bloody material and I couldn't read it and I said 'I cannot read it, man. It's gibberish.' And he said 'No, you've got to keep reading it and keep reading it.' and he says 'I tell ya, you'll come in one day and you'll just click.' So I started to read it – bit of Marx and a little bit of Engels.

ANNE: And I finished from Joyland School I went to a secondary school and I think that is where another chapter of my nightmare started. Being in Joyland, it was like a small heaven because everyone was disabled and they looked after us well. You know the classrooms, the dormitories, the…everything was accessible. And going to Cararey School, secondary school, it was just so difficult because I was moving on heavy callipers and crutches and to move from point A to B was just a nightmare for me. I kept falling down, the other students used to look at me and stare at me. It's like 'Why, what is she doing here?' and you know, things like that. So I had to sort of find a way to cope with this stigma…

NORMAN: But I realised about social injustice, about why was those people living there in that housing estate with horrible housing and stuff, while these other people who was living in big houses up in…

ANNE: My dad has always taught me that education was very important to everybody but it was more important for me because, being disabled, I could not just earn a living from doing manual work, you know. I couldn't do that. So my dad used to always tell me the only way you can survive this – you need to have an education.

NORMAN: Scargill…just people misunderstood to this day, they didn't understand Scargill. Yes he's got an ego, yes he's a huge ego but what he was saying was basically true. They're going t…if we don't fight they're going to close these pits down. And you've got a choice. Let them close them down, or fight.

ANNE: I couldn't access even the toilets, the bathrooms, the classrooms, you know, the laboratories. It, it was just so difficult, it was hell but I decided to, you know, toughen up. I had to decide whether I was going to quit or stay. And you know, just get on with it and that's what I did.

NORMAN: And in 1984 the miners' strike came along…ran for lodge office, union office, err got defeated by seven votes, probably because me names 'Strike' and err coz nobody wants to vote for a Strike. I was at Orgreave and the day I was at Orgreave err you know the big, the big day, Scargill was with me in the front as we're charging at the police. 'Come on lads,' 'No they've got horses,' 'They've got bigger horses at York racecourse, come on.'

ANNE: I just got on with life and erm, before I knew it the girls who were laughing at me… Suddenly they did not look at me as Anne with…legs and callipers and crutches, they just looked at me as Anne who was just another student, you know? And I was performing well, you know, better than them and that started giving me a bit of self-confidence and it raised my self-esteem because I knew, well at least if I can't challenge them in a different way, you know, we can compete academically.

NORMAN: And it was the saddest day of me life when I stood at the gates and all the men marched back in to go back to work, and they all went that way to get changed, and

I went that way, to get me final, ya know, me final pay
packet.

ANNE: And I remember when I was at the university, I think
I just blossomed you know as, as a person erm… I worked
so hard to fit in / and I was accepted by the other students
and I became very popular, you know, with the other
students erm…when I got my student's err merit award,
I was like 'Well there's no holding me back now, if I can
achieve this, you know, after all these troubles, you know,
I've achieved this, then I'm just as good as anybody else,'
you know?

NORMAN: And erm, I wrote to Portsmouth Polytechnic and
the admissions tutor asked to see me, she said ya know,
'So your dad was a miner,' she says 'You shouldn't be
anywhere near here, don't ya?' and she says, 'You don't
really meet the criteria but why do you want…?' I says 'I
want to read books,' 'Will you do me a favour?' she said,
'I'm going to take a chance with you, if after the first year
you're not cutting it would you leave without anybody
having to chuck you out?' and we made this deal. [And] I
became a teacher.

And err [then] I just decided I would go VSO. So they
sent me three jobs. The Maldives, Kenya…and what was
the other one? Maldives, Kenya and India. And I didn't
really fancy India because it was going to be teaching two
hundred kids at a time and I didn't really think I could
cope with that. The Maldives *(Makes sound.)* but then
when I looked at the Kenya one I thought, aw that looks,
ya know…they had a nice picture of a palm tree and I
thought that looks nice. If I'm going to go and do some
good for somebody, ya may as well do good for somebody
where it's nice and hot, eh?

ANNE: But after that I went to…in Kenya we call it fast
posting, this is after you finish your degree, they send you
to a school to be a teacher now so they, eh, The Teachers
Service Commission of Kenya send me to teach in this

place. Lenana High School. But when I got the student's merit award it was just fantastic because being at the university I was one of the students who regularly used to get invites to the chancellor's house to go for a meal and like when the other ministers came to the, to the university erm, we had, had to go and perform…like you know some songs and I'd play the piano, you know, and I was very popular, you know and…

NORMAN: Probably because you had such a good voice.

ANNE: And after some, I think after teaching for about two years, that's when I met Norman. I met you at a party. And the first thing, no…it's funny, he was sitting somewhere inside the room and I walked, I walked in on my callipers and crutches.

NORMAN: No…wrong story

ANNE: Oh, were you sitting outside?

NORMAN: I was sitting outside coz it was so hot and I was…

ANNE: Oh yeh, you were sitting outside.

NORMAN: Holding a vodka bottle.

ANNE: Yeh, yeh…

NORMAN: And you appeared in the doorway.

ANNE: I appeared in the doorway and the first thing he say, 'Oh did you break your legs skiing?' And I was like…

NORMAN: Good chat up line that, weren't it?

ANNE: And I was like, what's wrong with him, you know? You know, skiing in Kenya. And then I said, 'No.' I said actually I had polio and he was so embarrassed, isn't it?

NORMAN: I was going, 'Oh for… Oh, blooming heck, sorry ey… Eeee sorry.'

ANNE: Yeh, he really did. He was sort of embarrassed.

NORMAN: Oh I thought she was the most beautiful thing I'd ever seen in me life.

Enter ROGER BLACK, he addresses the audience.

ROGER: I was always the fastest kid in the school, always. … I could run fast from a very early age, there's no doubt about it. And um, I wasn't, I mean this, it wasn't that I was fast, I was miles faster than anybody else. …

So, I had this talent but I had no desire to be an athlete. My dad was a doctor…so I went for medicine. And I got, and I actually didn't get in because I, I messed up my maths A-Level exam. And that was the biggest shock of my life – devastated. And it was probably, at that time, no doubt the best day of my life because that was the day my life was shaped.

A friend of mine…convinced me to join Hampshire Athletics Club and give it a go because two guys had just come back from the '84 Olympics, Kriss Akabusi and Todd Bennett…

Started training, in a great group down in Southampton and two months later got my first international vest.

SLIDE PROJECTED.

Slide text 'Geri Buckley, Pistol shooter. Since interview Geri's training continues but she has not qualified to London 2012 – focus now Rio 2016'.

GERI: …so you create a performance profile, a check list really – if you can do all these things you can be an Olympic Champion. So you break that down into different trigger training exercises you can do. How smoothly you release the trigger… So I might spend an hour and a half one day not even firing a shot…all I'm doing is focusing on how smoothly I pull the trigger. It sounds ridiculously boring, but you know you appreciate the benefit of these monotonous exercises…

SLIDE PROJECTED.

Slide text 'Simon Wilson. Wheelchair fencing. Selected London 2012.'

SIMON: ...and I said 'I don't consider myself disabled.' And he said 'Have you ever thought of wheelchair fencing?'

'Don't want to do it, not at any price. I don't need the label, don't need the wheelchair. Don't want to do it.'

And he says 'Well you're a prat. 'Cos you'd be good.'... So I came in February 2007 and by May I was in the GB squad.

SCENE 5

CHARMIAN is raised above the stage, as though on a high diving board. An image of black water is projected.

CHARMIAN: I had no coach – no full-time coach. I was geographically misplaced. There was a man... Erm, I do not acknowledge this man, but he was there when I started to dive. He was the reason I gave up diving. He was not honest with me, he...and it wasn't long before I knew more about diving than he did. I have a scar here where I hit the diving board, erm, because I didn't get away from the board because I hadn't been taught properly how to do it.

Spider, John Webb, Spider we used to call him, he was on the poolside, now if I'd been with him, he'd have been a good coach and er he said he would yell out in the right place and when he yelled out I just went 'tunk' you know just opened for the water erm, I went straight up to the ten metres and I did the dive, and Spider yelled out and I knew that, yes I'd done the dive again, safely, but I knew that if he hadn't yelled out, I could've done the same thing again.

Yes, yes I remember erm, pre-nineteen-fifty-two.

Sees a rabbit.

Oh there's a rabbit, I have a pair of rabbits in the garden, he's just gone into the hedge, erm... I ...every time I saw a new moon I used to bow three times and say 'I wish, I wish a jolly good wish, I wish my wish come true, I wish to go to the Olympic games!'

I used to wish that, yes. But I was very sup, I was very superstitious I still am really. One of the things they used to do, know this r s, RSPCA dogs? Used to pat it on the head and put a copper in the box...whenever I passed one.

SLIDE PROJECTED.

Slide text 'Charmian Rawlings née Welsh. Diver. Fifth place, Helsinki Olympics 1952.'

But about Helsinki, it was the fifteenth Olympiad of the modern era.

When I was competing, sport in this country was considered a pastime, an evening pastime, because we all had to work, we all had to make a living, Erm, it, professionalism, was frowned on... I remember in, I don't know which year it was, but we were pretty young still...swimming in Redcar and the prize was, erm, half-a-crown's worth of savings stamps. Now technically that could've made me a professional, half-a-crown. What's that now, erm, ten fifteen pence? That could've made me a professional.

SLIDE PROJECTED.

Slide text 'Beth Davidson. Fencer. Commonwealth Games Gold medallist. England Team Manager.'

BETH: I am the North East's Regional Development Officer for, uh, the North East obviously, but also in my other capacities I am the England Team Manager and Junior, uh, Junior Great British Sabre Manager... As well as a selector.

CHARMIAN: Gosh how things have changed.

BETH: Ahhh. This Olympics is…it's, it's become an event beyond an event. Um…uh, I mean for some people it's… we have very young athletes who get into the sport, and in fencing you can actually succeed within the sport within your own country very quickly. It's a small sport and with any sort of input and nuance you can get a ranking…um, and to young people, and parents especially, they get these very big delusions that the more money and more, um, uh, pressure to, uh, they just see themselves that they can suddenly qualify for the Olympics.

CHARMIAN: Well, that you've got to go back to what Coubertin said in the first place, er, it, the honour was taking part in it, er I can't remember his exact words but er the honour was just taking part, not necessarily for anything you can gain from it. But I say you need to do research on that.

BETH: …and, um, and some parents are just so deluded that they will use the officials, abuse the officials, and just bulldozer over them to try and achieve that and, you know, I've personally been working with an athlete for a number of years who, you know she's fairly, fairly nice potentially, she's a handy person, um. But, the parents, um, they're just, well, trying to bulldoze her through that and they don't care who they stamp on, I don't get paid for that.

CHARMIAN: Erm, I heard that one of the athletes, the top athletes, refused to come to, to, to, to put in…to show up at a particular event because the money she was offered was not enough. That I think is sad. You know, when you have to be paid just to be there, that I think is sad. But er…

BETH: But in the end the Olympics is, you know, it becomes, you know, it's not about the sport anymore.

I mean I was actually in a position to, to team manage an athlete who was selected, well who qualified for the Olympics, not from here – overseas, uh, a very good friend, and she qualified for her national team – outright, she achieved the benchmark that was set in front of her, and effectively [not naming names] her place was sold to another much wealthier country. She's very similar to me, we're very close friends and our approach to fencing was always the same and we trained and...

BETH is upset.

I hate feeling like this... I should have just stayed home today.

CHARMIAN: Shall I make some more coffee?

BETH: [So you see] when you're in the sport and when you're sort of, um, an athlete and absolutely you've got, you know, the Olympics as a pull but sometimes it's... and also the politics in sport now is just immense, hugely immense...and the athletes need someone to be a still point for them, someone who knows what it's like – who's been there. That's my role. And all this...this politics this other stuff it's my job to soak it up and be the one who knows what it's like – to be on the edge for them so they don't have to be there. I've been trusted to lead these athletes at this time because I've been successful in my England activity, Common Wealth Games, World Championships...and I can coach them because of that experience.

There's not many people out there, in day-to-day life who can say they've been to a World Championships, European Championships, a world class event and been part of it, and been able to compete for your country, not many people can say that, but I can, and so every competition I felt it was a privilege to be there and uh, I wanted to give it my all, um to do that.

I'm proud of my success but I know what it costs them to operate at that level, for myself, I felt that pressure at the end of my elite career.

I think... I just said, you know the efforts to get in, to get out, the balance was all wrong, and so I made the decision to use the Commonwealth Games in Belfast to be my swan song and I told everybody I was retiring after that and you know everybody was really sweet…but retiring it's hard… it was like death in the family.

BETH is upset.

ROGER: I mean, you retire from this thing that's consumed you…you don't have a balanced life. I could give you a list of great Olympic athletes, who've all been divorced and it's a hell of a list.

BETH: The family thing does bug me. That does bug me because I've only got a small family anyhow. So the family thing does bug me and I think er…yeah and that choice…when I made the choice to stop being that elite performer time was starting to become more compressed. You know, to have a family? Erm, so yeah…that, that, that, *(Sigh.)* you know, that's life isn't it? So you…you know it's something I'm focusing on now but you know trying to find somebody to do it with. That sounds rather…

ROGER: …because there's that ego that comes in, that's needed for high level performance. … So you may have relationships but you're not going to have proper ones. And so you…you…y'know, it makes you a bit of a wanker, if I'm honest, and emotionally void in most cases which I was.

BETH has taken up a sabre and fencing mask (or there is the suggestion of this equipment). She is joined by KIRA in a fencing mask.

BETH: Fencing, its purity is very simple. Fencing is about trying to hit a person faster and earlier than the other person can hit you. … OK…so this is what Kira's gonna do, is just do a…a movement by the feet to shorten the distance and hit me on the head which is target area for sabre

KIRA does.

…and now she's going to do a step and lunge and hit me on another part of the body because she's hit me on the head and I'm gonna think 'Right when she attacks again I'm gonna protect my head.' So I do a defensive move called parry –

They fence.

So I'm sort of thinking… I could use another system where I could make her miss me…

KIRA: Can I use a system as well?

BETH: What's that?

KIRA: Can I use a system as well?

BETH: No, you're going to be a loser all the time.

They both laugh.

BETH: So this time she's gonna try and hit me again.

They fence. BETH hits KIRA.

And I make her miss and I try and hit her back again… er…let's have a think. OK, I'll do the movement…

KIRA: Why don't we do that scenario…and I think of things to do as well and then they can see how complicated it can get? Because we're both thinking of things, yeah…

BETH: OK. We'll try attacking each other. We'll do the circle of…the tactical circle.

KIRA: OK, so I'll start from basic…

BETH: We'll start from the first one where we both try to hit each other as fast as possible. So it's just simultaneous.

They fence. KIRA hits BETH. Laughter from both.

OK. So I thought I was intelligent fencer but she realised that and she changed it round again. So we sort of start again at the beginning again.

SLIDE PROJECTED.

Slide text 'Kira Roberts. Fencer. Graduated Durham University rising through the rankings, Commonwealth Gold medal – but not qualified for 2012 – focused on Rio 2016'.

KIRA: My mum, when I started fencing, was…that she used to get really, really angry as well…and like it was kind of like a shouting match afterwards…and she was like 'Why did you do so badly?' 'Don't know! Don't know! Why are you just shouting at me?' and she was like 'Don't know!' 'Why are shouting at me?' and she was…and it would like go and on and on and escalate. And at one stage I just couldn't have her next to the piste when I was fencing because I'd just find that so distracting…there's so much expectation.

SLIDE PROJECTED.

Slide text 'James McLean. 110m hurdler. Did not qualify for London 2012.'

JAMES: I have to be more balanced than that. I think I probably seen what can happen if you're too selfish but I think there's other things that are so much more important than…like your family and that…but for athletics to be number one you have to…but you wouldn't be happy if you was, if you wasn't happy at home…it's all been drilled into you… Everybody in UK Athletics is thinking about 2012. I don't think looking beyond that is feasible.

SCENE 6

ROGER enters and addresses the audience.

ROGER: [The] golden hopefuls who are young…um…athletes of different sports who are all trying to get to 2012. One might, most won't. It's not the point. It's the journey. And my job is to be on that journey with them.

KAT: Erm, my name's Katherine Copeland and I'm in the light weight women's doubles sculls boat erm, and we've done trials all through the year and then seat racing which is in crew boats, erm, and I, got in instead of Hester, so now it'll be me and Sophie who go to the Olympics.

RACHEL: I've always had like a secret hope but I'm still not qualified yet. The qualification regatta is in Lucerne next weekend. And, it's going to be like a massive task, like it's going to, require me to row at my very best…

ROGER: Um, in the same breathe we're all different, you know? I'm not a young guy with an Asian background with no legs. So as much as I can talk about going to the Olympics and all that sort of stuff, I'm not Ali. So you know…

ALI: Well, I was about six when I watched the Atlanta Olympic Games, that was my first memory of the Olympic Games and err, my first memory was Roger Black. Which was very, fairly ironic now but it was Roger Black in the 400 metre final and erm I saw like Michael Johnson winning it and then afterwards getting his medal and like the emotion on his face made me realise I have to be there.

The girls start rowing. KAT describing the action as they row.

KAT: So you would like, leg press it, lean back and then go with your arms, but because it accelerates through the water by the time it gets to you, pulling your arms in to take the blades / out it.

They row.

ALI: No, they er, I think, I was born in Lebanon but erm because I had a disability, they really didn't have a clue there so it was going to be…it wasn't going to be a very good life so they decided to go elsewhere…so I'd get a better life…coz, err, I came out like this and nobody… it was a shock to a lot of people. Especially my parents because the scan said that I was fine. So they thought, ya know, I was a healthy baby and then I came out, with no legs. It was a shock. So the doctors actually offered to err, ya know, kill me. Luckily my parents loved me enough to err keep me…so…

Both girls stop rowing to talk.

KAT: It's not as, I, you're not as sociable as you would be if you weren't training, like you go places but you / don't really…

RACHEL: You see anything but the lake.

KAT: …like people have been to some amazing places like Australia and places but you never really, you only see like the hotel and the lake, the hotel and the lake like… [RACHEL: Yeah.] or you get to…

RACHEL: Go sunbathe or anything

The girls start rowing again.

ALI: So they decided to err, come here. Because like here, they offer like legs and plastic legs and stuff. I was a refugee for eleven years, I think. So I came here when I was six months old and I got it when I was about eleven.

The girls stop rowing.

RACHEL: Yeah.

KAT: …walk around Italy and I just think you are quite, and because it's quite like, mentally draining as well I don't, yeah you almost feel a bit like, not stunted but, [RACHEL: It's…] I think like, socially and like, not even like I don't but just like mentally outside of rowing I don't, don't really think about a lot else.

RACHEL: Yeah, it's / the type

KAT: So it is like you're in a little bubble.

The girls start rowing.

ALI: Err, yeh. Erm, my parents always thought that I should be in mainstream. They never thought that I should be in a special school so… Really enjoyed it actually. Nobody bullied me, nobody teased me. They treated me, you know, the same, which is good. I was one of the popular ones, it was really weird. Like, you know, you see this old person, as a kid you think, you're actually quite curious, you go up and talk to them, where you don't really care. But like when you're older, you think you know, you recognise when there's something wrong with you, what's wrong.

The girls stop rowing.

KAT: When I was in primary school I was really chubby, didn't do any sport or, erm, yeah er, wasn't sporty at all. I didn't even know how to play rounders like…

RACHEL: I remember meeting Kat in the toilets one day and I was, I've always been very tall and I used to be a / swimmer so already into my sport and…

KAT: I just said you're really big you should try rowing, cos in general I mean, well, I'm not a very good example but I do light weight rowing but in general like, a lot of rowers are tall, big [RACHEL: Long levers they are.] people, yeah long levers that's what they look for. Yeah.

RACHEL: I remember, I used to really want to be a marine biologist, cos like I used to read this series of books, like I can't even remember what they were called now, but it was always /about dolphins

KAT: Erm, a hairdresser, but like that was when, I think like, all little girls go through a phase of wanting to be something like…

The girls start rowing.

ALI: I used to play a lot of football when I was younger, like I really enjoyed it. Well, you've seen me like crawl around, haven't you? Well, I can run really fast. And I can like… people and shoot with my hands. So I used to run on tarmac and you know, played lots of football. It was good. I actually said to my mum 'I want to be a footballer.' she goes like 'You can't, you've got no legs.' I was like 'Really?' I was like really shocked.

The girls rowing. They keep rowing as KAT describes the action.

KAT: …it's actually quite a loose movement because the handles are already moving so fast and your arms you, well your arms are nowhere near as strong enough as your legs…

They continue rowing.

ALI: And it was proper old, spit and sawdust gym where you don't… I didn't think I belonged there to be honest. … So err, we're on the bench and there was this old man kept looking at me and it really bugged me that there was this old man looking at me. I thought he was like a pervert or something. I started benching and I think my first bench was like 100 kilo which was very, very good at that age. This old man came up to me afterwards and he's like erm 'What's your name?' I was like oh God he's scary… He's like 'What about, you know, maybe continuing to come to the gym?' I was like 'No, no I'm not very strong.'

He's like 'Yeh but I think you've got the potential to make the Paralympic Games, maybe.' I was like 'What?' He goes 'You know, on the bench press.'… So when he said that, I had to go and reconsider it. I was like, well you know, if I'm good at this I could, if I give it everything, I could make you know the next, well not Beijing, but the next Olympics after that.

The girls rowing.

RACHEL: No that's right, / you're in your own bubble…

KAT: It's like you're in this bubble and it's like, you get up, and you go training just to Caversham and then you come back and you're literally like you don't, you don't do that much for the rest of the day cos it's all like, you have to be recovered.

RACHEL: Yeah, it's like being at / school.

They row.

ALI: I just like rocketed up without, you know, couldn't believe how quick I improved. And I set a British record that hadn't been broken for 25 years, at a senior level, not a junior level.

The girls rowing, KAT speaks as she rows.

KAT: Yeah, like the basics of it, cos a lot of people think it's with your arms you have to have really strong arms but it's not it's like, most of it is just like your bum and your legs / erm, so.

They row.

ALI: And it was on my birthday that I qualified…for Beijing. Well, I, to be honest, I got there, really excited, really expecting to have a really good time. Err, a lot of the senior guys said to me I won't enjoy it because it can be very boring. I was like 'What are you talking about, it's an Olympic Games.'

The girls stop rowing to speak.

RACHEL: …but, your body just works on autopilot and before you know it you're at training and just like, used to it.

KAT: Sounds horrible but like it is good…

RACHEL: Yeah.

KAT: It is good. It's not like ah / boo hoo

They start rowing.

ALI: And I think three days before the competition I bench pressed, you know, a huge PB. I thought right this is, you know. 190, yeh. Especially at that age, I was like, this is really good. Like I knew it weren't going to get me a medal, but it could get me fifth place. And erm, I think it was at the evening before? Yeh, the evening before the competition I felt really sick, and I called the doctor, got me in. He said 'It's only a head cold, don't worry about it.' I was like to him 'My stomach is killing me, this is not a head cold, this is something else.' Overnight I got really bad, overnight and erm I got to the competition. I thought, I can't do it, you know, literally…

The girls rowing as KAT describes the action.

KAT: So you can't actually really add anything to it by then, it's just sort of happened and then, yeah you just repeat again so move your arms and your body away and, up the slide.

They row.

ALI: …I was that sick I was going to pull out, but the coach said 'Look, you've done incredible just to get here.' He goes 'Take it.' He goes, 'There's no pressure on you, you're still a little boy, you're a baby, you know, 2012 will be your time.' So… I came ninth eventually but, very disappointed. But err my condition got worse, it got worse.

The girls rowing.

RACHEL: You know of course it feels like everything right now, but um…but you know I'm happy at the minute, I'm quite happy in, in the little rowing land.

The girls smile.

SLIDE PROJECTED.

Slide text 'Rachel Gamble-Flint. Rower. Finished sixth in Regatta in Lucern. Failed to qualify for London 2012.'

They row.

ALI: When I came back into training things weren't going too well, I got worse. So they erm, went inside me, to see what was wrong and it turned out to be err Crohn's Disease. Have you heard of that? It's probably the worst disease you could ever have. You can't digest food properly, and any food that you do digest, you just get loads of ulcers that will bleed and that bleeding will just make you have all these other symptoms. I think, in Beijing that's what it was, well it must have been the start of it but I didn't realise and

I got misdiagnosed then…so… I got a very bad hand to play so…

ROGER enters.

ROGER: It was just momentum. Everything I did just, just sort of got better and better and better. Everything I did I just improved. But there was a reason for that. I hadn't got injured yet. And then suddenly you get injured and it changes everything. It changes everything. So after, I won the Commonwealth and Europeans in '86, British record holder, sky's the limit, next year broke my foot.

I was in plaster for ten weeks and…and that's what, that's where you really find out. Ultimately three years to get back, for me. It was a long time. The reason that so many people don't come back from injury is that a doctor just says that'll be healed in six weeks. So you think, right, six weeks time, great. Of course, it doesn't go like that.

And it was never in doubt for me that I would carry on. I read all the books on self-development and self-improvement and all that sort of stuff because you can, and started to sort of really think about it er, had to make changes, changed my coach. It was tough, really tough but I got back. I would have been twenty…twenty-one, twenty-two. So…

Makes a whooshing noise.

…and then bang. Straight down. Straight in, straight down. And then the rest of my career.

SLIDE PROJECTED.

Slide text 'Alyson Dixon. Marathon runner. Since interview won Brighton Marathon. Qualified World Championships in Daegu – suffered injured foot. Not qualified for London 2012.'

ALYSON: So just…it does take over your life anything from a 110 miles to 120 miles a week. Like a Saturday I do two training sessions and…we'll go to the cinema…but there's no kind of like relaxing, oh kind of nip down to one of the bars cos I'm like always scared that someone is going to stand on my foot and that's it – game over.

SLIDE PROJECTED.

Slide Text: 'Freya Murray. Marathon and long distance runner. Ran first Marathon at London and was the second British athlete home with only one remaining place for the marathon... Failed to qualify for London 2012.'

FREYA: ...hopefully I've got another, at least another, ten years in me or so...whether I'll still be doing it in ten years time is another matter like... Steve always says you're only a hamstring away from oblivion *(Laughs.)* you never know what's going to happen next *(Laughs.)* so erm, like, it's so... It's such a difficult...

SCENE 7

ANNE: I'm not a good storyteller.

NORMAN: Just, yeh... *(Mumbles.)*

ANNE: Oh God, I don't think my, mine is not as interesting as Norman...

Laughs.

NORMAN: Of course, it's much more interesting Anne, much more interesting.

ANNE: I'm not a good speaker, the way, sort of, yeh um... Yeh, we just got chatting and then [NORMAN: She didn't like me much.] I, I didn't like him and his accent was strange coz he's from England and to me his English didn't sound like the Queen's English. You know the English that I used to listen to on the BBC? His English was very different and he say to me 'Geordie' and I was like 'So what part of Europe is that?' You know? And yeh, he started explaining to me, you know, different accents, you know of England and all that but the first time I met him he sounded strange…yeh.

NORMAN: And I've continued to do so.

ANNE: Yeh, but it's sort of, they say that's how people from the North East spoke yeh? But [NORMAN: I explained that I was a posh Geordie *(ANNE is laughing.)* coz my accent's been toned down by 25 years.] It's because you've been in the South is it? Yeh. But, yeh, I sort of got to like his sense of humour and after some time, you know, after several, I don't know, after how long I sort of thought, he's intelligent and he's humorous, you know? And I thought 'Oh, he's, he's not very bad,' you know? But, you know, still it's funny, I said this to Norman, still after achieving all you know, getting an education and all that I sort of still, there was other things I missed doing. You know like dancing or you know, I couldn't get on the dance floor and dance. It's funny because erm, when I started going out with Norman this one time when he was drunk, he actually was pulling me to get on the dance floor to dance with him, remember?

NORMAN crosses to ANNE.

NORMAN: I was more disabled than you were!

ANNE: No but, yeh, you were drunk, you were drunk.

ANNE is laughing.

NORMAN: Well, I've always been a terrible dancer. I mean there's no… I'm awful. But I went and tried to dance…

ANNE: Yeh, we tried to dance…

NORMAN: I nearly knocked you over though, didn't I?

ANNE: I think so, yeh. Yeh, I was standing on callipers and crutches and he's trying to make me dance, yeh. Yeh, but it's really interesting because erm, I think after I met Norman we started writing to each other, isn't it, and then you started phoning me and what you used to do, you

used to climb, you used to climb, you know, on top of the
ceiling, to go into the headmaster's office when, where he
used to teach, to steal the phone, the telephone…

NORMAN: The headmaster had a telephone in his office that
was locked in a box – coz it's Kenya right? But I found out
if you, there was a gap between the library and his office,
and I could crawl through… I'd phone Anne up and we'd
have long conversations on the school phone.

ANNE: But they used to get huge bills, like they never knew
where the bills came from.

NORMAN: It's not like here where you get an itemised bill.
They would just get these bills and they'd 'How on earth
are we using all this money on…?'

ANNE: Yeh, yeh and we, we got engaged but I remember
the first time I introduced Norman to my family. I've
got a cousin of mine, he passed away. As soon as he saw
Norman he was like, he started negotiating for dowry.

NORMAN: He said, 'Excuse me, can I have a chat with you?'
He was this big tall bloke and he had a pink suit on, you
know, big tall African bloke in a pink suit. And I said,
'Yes.' He said 'Ahh, it's my job to…you like Anne?' I said
'Yes.' He said 'Ahh, I want to talk to you about dowry.' I
said 'Dowry? What's that?' He said, 'Well she's an educated
girl and if you want to marry her…' I said 'I've only just
met her!'

ANNE: Yeh, and then later he came and told me, 'I've just
asked for fifteen cattle of, you know, but I think you are
worth more than that because you've got a degree.'

NORMAN: They appointed this new disciplinary headmaster
and he was caning the kids in front of the school and it
was driving me… I was trying to get the other teachers
to, to, to, to, you know? Rise up and stop it and they
wouldn't, they thought it was wrong but they wouldn't
and eventually he just caned this girl and I just grabbed
the cane off him and I said, 'If you touch one more kid

I'm going to wrap this round your friggin' neck, d'ya understand that?' And he was like shocked and didn't do it. But I got sacked but she still had a term to go. Anne said 'Can we go to England?' I said, 'Ya don't want to go to England man, it's horrible.' She said 'No I want to have a look.' I said 'Ya don't man, honestly, trust me, ya don't want to go to England.' She says, 'I would like to just go to have a look.' I said, 'You wouldn't, Anne.' She says, 'Honest.' I said, 'Alright then,' I said, 'But don't say I didn't tell ya.' And the plan was she'd come back to England for two years, we'd save up some more money on top of the little bit money that we had and then we'd go back to Kenya, we'd buy a house, she would become a headmistress and I'd sit on the veranda and write novels.

ROGER BLACK enters and addresses the audience.

ROGER: And it was fun. The reason I didn't do it at school was 'cause it was not fun. The reason I did it was because I joined a training group with people like Kriss Akabusi who are amazing fun, Daley Thompson, these guys are amazing. It was like hanging out with your mates every day, doing a bit of running. It was brilliant. It was great. It was no sacrifice, no sacrifice at all, none. And any athlete who ever says they sacrificed, no you didn't, no you didn't. It wasn't a sacrifice, you were lucky to have the chance. No sacrifice. It was fantastic.

SLIDE PROJECTED.

Slide text 'John Mayock. Middle distance runner. Commonwealth Games Silver medallist, European Indoor Championship, Gold Medallist. Competed in 1996 Atlanta, 2000 Sydney and 2004 Athens Olympics.'

JOHN: I've trained for fifteen years to get to the Olympic Games – since I was ten, eleven years old. All that training and training twice a day, every day, giving up so much of your life when all your mates have been going to the pub and girlfriends and nightclubs and you've done none of that, you know? I've got to do it, you know…

SCENE 8

Enter VIV MILLS.

VIV: And I went into the competition and absolutely knocked seven bells out of the Poles to begin with, and then fenced the Russians and I hit this Russian woman, and I riposted so fast…and I whipped the weapon in and it pinged round the side of her face mask and as it did so it caught the clip…and it took it round the back of her face mask and buried it in the back of her head. And that was…yeah, but what an amazing shot. What an amazing shot! And I said to the ref 'Do I get an extra point for that? Cos that was…drawn blood actually drawn blood from doing that amazing shot.' 'No Certainly not!' Hmm yeah so…so I was well sui… I picked the right weapon you see.

ALI: I went back to the specialist and he said you know 'I really think you should consider retiring…because you're never going to be one hundred per cent, you know, you compete at a world class level, this puts you at a major disadvantage.'

You know, I was seriously thinking about suicide and everything. Because the medication that I'm on it makes you want to kill yourself, it's really that bad.

VIV: Um… I was um… I was abducted as a child. Quite an episode in my life. I've never discussed it with anybody… erm… I was abducted. I had my younger brother with me…and erm, by a man who it later transpired had just come out of prison having done something similar, erm… and um…it's funny cos I… I was six-years-old. And erm… I managed to escape, the guy tried to drag me off into a wood. I got my brother… I got my baby brother in a push chair and erm…and I escaped. And a police car came, and it happened to be a dog handler…with a dog…and I was able to identify a witness…and I gave a full description of this man and his moustache his build his height everything about him… I'd given them a full description…and they caught this guy. I thought 'This is a job this is.' And when

they said to me 'What do you want to do for a career?'
I thought 'Well, this is what I wanna do – bit of that.'
Interviewing people, arresting people, going out in a car
with a dog... Yeah let's have a bit of this.

[So later] I finished my A levels on a Friday afternoon and
on the Monday morning I started as a Police cadet. And
that was the start of police career.

ALI: That day...so that day I thought [when I went home]
I thought 'That's it. I'm not going back.' I'd had enough.
But...ever since I was a kid, if I believed in something that
much, I'd give everything for, until I do it. No matter what
the odds are. Or the pain was. So I decided to go back to
lifting again.

VIV: ...so at the age of twenty-four I was the youngest
inspector, not just in my county, but probably in the
country. Which was quite an accolade...then I was
promoted to Superintendent down here in Sussex.

ALI: And then my condition got a lot worse err last year, in
about January time. I'd eaten something that I shouldn't
have. It turned out to be a little bit raw. Obviously...it was
err salmon...ended up inflaming my intestine and causing
a lot of infection. Got rushed into hospital, needed an
operation, to take it, to take half my intestine out. I was like
'Oh God, here we go.'

VIV: It was a Friday afternoon. It was a bank holiday weekend.
I'd been at work. A very, very hot day similar to today
and er I was due to go and visit one of my officers who'd
been off sick for a long time – he'd had surgery on his
back. He didn't want to retire on ill health he said 'I really
want to come back to work.' So I said 'Well, I'll come
and talk to you about it.' And I called in here and had a
shower and got changed and as I went out the front door
I heard an alarm go off in that house over there... Err, so
I...whizzed round and was there within 30 seconds and
found a window open err, an upstairs window open and
erm, I couldn't find a key holder anywhere and I'd called

it in and asked for back up. Back up arrived and the guy from next door came round and said I've got a nice big ladder.' So we got the ladder out of his garage. And we put the ladder up against the window. And I went up the ladder and as I was climbing in through the window, I took a blow to the top of my head and I fell backwards out of the window. That was that… That was the end of my career. That was the end of everything…really in terms of policing. And erm I spent the next seventh months in hospital and erm came out in a wheelchair.

ALI: So I was like 'Oh God.' So I said to them 'What do you think are the odds?' They went 'There is no way,' he said 'You could die in this operation, this is dangerous. You know, there's no way you should even think about competing.' Obviously with me I totally ignored that and was thinking about the training. He didn't like that. I was like 'Yeh, you just do your job and I'll do mine.' So after the operation, I came out of it, I think it was about six hours later and I said to the nurses, 'Was it successful?' She said, 'You're a very lucky boy.' she goes, 'You have to look after yourself now.' But I thought, you know 'I've got bigger fish to fry, you know, 2012 is still there.' So… I started training again.

VIV: My Chief Constable visited me at home told me I was no use to anyone and they couldn't get…couldn't get rid of me fast enough so they pensioned me off. So… I decided that I would learn to walk, so I put all my energies into that.

ALI: Yet again my body was failing me. My bodyweight then was up to 75 kilo but now because err, I've been very sick for a couple of years and I'm back down to about 51 now. I've lost a lot of weight…went back to the Specialist erm, had some blood tests and…

VIV: Four years ago I was watching this documentary with Tanni Grey-Thompson about the Beijing Olympics. The Chinese put together a Paralympic team of 600 athletes and I thought 'We should do the same in London'. The only way we are going to do this if is every disabled person who is fit puts their name forward. So I suddenly thought 'This means you – you're fit – you've got four years to do a sport and get into the Paralympic team. So what are you going to do?'

So I thought 'Well, I don't even know what…you know what sports they do. I've seen them doing athletics and I've seen people whizzing up and down a track in…' I sort of watched to see…because if we don't have somebody doing this sport maybe we haven't got anybody qualified or maybe nobody does that sport or whatever…so I've probably got a better chance of making the team…so I thought 'Right well, fencing, it looks like it's gonna be fencing.'

I mean erm, I started to learn the sort of the finer points of my nice little deft touches with my sabre but you know the first thing I learned was to give someone a good whack with it.

ALI: …and it turned out that I… it has come back worse. It's come back worse than before. So I've been out for six weeks. I just have to make sure this time you know, that I don't get stressed about it and just err keep looking forward.

VIV: So I've been fencing for Great Britain just over a year. I qualified for the World Championships in November. And erm… I almost did Britain proud – I came seventh…but that's not bad for your first world championships.

[It was going pretty well.] But they've decided there's no sabre in the Paralympics next year so I've had to change from doing sabre to doing foil. Sounds simple, but it's a different weapon, a different technique. I've trained in one discipline and…and that change over I'm… I'm finding it a little bit hard. I was in contention and now it's a bit like starting all over again.

ALI: So, I've still got a shot, and I may do it next year. But it won't be a medal next year, I don't think. I'll just have to hope that I get there and just perform for my country rather than expecting a medal.

VIV: Right well… The decision will be made in twelve months time – who is gonna go to the Paralympics. And erm, so all of us those of us who are eligible are all fencing and fighting one another for those places and err… At the moment the focus is London… Yes. It dominates everything. Even to the point where I don't go and do physio on my legs at the moment. I do a little bit but not enough. And I'm slightly worried that my legs are starting to deteriorate a bit.

ALI: I cannot afford to be sick again. If that happens I won't make it next year. I think this has to be the last time I've flared up. If it happens again, I won't make it, because you I've just lost too much ground.

VIV: Cos I've already planned where I'm going with the walking scenario. Because I always said, right from the outset, I would learn to walk, before I pop my clogs, I will be able to walk unaided. And I'm still determined that that will be the case. That I will be able to walk unaided before I'm finished. But where the answer lies is stem cell therapy.

Erm and while we wait for science to…to do its business and to develop embryonic stem cells erm, and to get embryonic stem cells to do what it is we want them to do – while they're doing that – I'm doing my fencing. And when they've decided this works that's when I'll step in and say 'I'll have a bit of that please,' and then when I can walk again – that'll be great and then I can keep teaching the fencing. And then maybe even teach able-bodied by that time. So that's my plan. But the focus is London…the focus is London…

SLIDE PROJECTED.

Slide text 'Viv Mills. Wheelchair fencer. Failed to qualify London 2012. Now focused on World Championships.'

ROGER: Talent is a, is a gift and I think, I think most Olympians have been given a gift...doesn't mean they're going to make it. It means that they can just, they've got an aptitude for it.

ALI: And I think, I dinnar, I felt this, I thought, right OK you need to get I... I'm quite a calm person, but I need to get really, really angry. So I went out on the platform... I was in my own little daze. I couldn't even see the crowd. I got on there, it was like a blank, there was nobody there. It was weird, all I could hear was like voices and loads of shouting but I really couldn't see anybody.

But I thought right, you can't, you can't you know s... you know, you can't give up. You know, you know you're capable. All you have to do is believe that you are capable. So I thought I have to make, I have to imagine that this is the ceiling trying to cave in and I have to push it away. That's what, that's what I thought, I had to you know, push the ceiling away from collapsing the ceiling, or I'll die.

SLIDE FADES IN

Slide text 'Ali Jawad. Powerlifter. 9ᵗʰ Beijing Olympic 2008. Qualified for London 2012.'

And I eventually like, it went really slow but I was just fighting every step of the way. And all I could hear was just like a voice, like proper shouting. It was incredible. And I got it up eventually and I got a few white lights and I was jumping. Like I was, I was proper jumping...because I knew I did it. That's probably the best moment.

SCENE 9

Enter ROGER. He addresses the audience.

ROGER: I made up a tape, actually. And it's all the words in the songs. A lot of Aztec Camera er, Tears for Fears, only… the biggest phrase was for me, an Aztec Camera song when the line was, 'The secret is silver and it's to shine and never simply survive' which is, was always for me, you know, the secret in life is to shine and not just to survive and you know…and that was true in sport because…

ROGER prepares a pair of walkman headphones.

…you know, we're all talented, we're all good but it wasn't about surviving it was about shining.

As ROGER puts on his headphones the music; Aztec Camera, builds.

Enter WILL and HILARY, as music fades. WILL is an Olympic torchbearer.

WILL: I know I'll be running about three hundred metres?

HILARY: I think so yeah.

WILL: But I don't know how quick I'm supposed to be doing it. Err, which is a bit scary because I'd quite like to know and err, I don't know where I'm going to carry it yet. When do I find out about that?

HILARY: I think, I think next month.

WILL: Yeah, next month and, erm, erm…

HILARY: Well, New/castle, yeah…

WILL: Newcastle but, erm, it, I'm not sure exactly where erm, but I'm a bit worried in case I drop it or it goes out of something.

SLIDE FADES IN

Slide text 'Will Hardy. Swimmer and Olympic Torch Bearer.'

WILL: Err, well I'll have to see how heavy it is, but erm, no I'm hoping to walk it, just to walk it, just on my normal legs.

HILARY: Do you want to tell your story about what happened and how you, how things are?

SLIDE FADES IN

Slide text 'Hilary Hardy. Will's mum.'

WILL: Well, er, when I was 'bout two?

HILARY: Yeah, twenty-three months.

WILL: Two. When I was two erm, I had meningitis and I lost my legs and one of my arms. That's pretty much it really. I was probably far too young to remember it.

HILARY addresses the following to WILL, indicating the relevant parts of his body.

HILARY: What happens is, well your body is, is fighting really hard against that infection and it fights to keep your vital organs going, your brain and your heart and things, and so it shuts down on the peripheries like the out…the edges of your body. Which is why people lose their limbs and why this bit of your ear went.

Touches his ear.

Cos that's just on the edge. And you have just this hand sticking out of a bandage and we watched it over those first few hours just to see whether it would stop. They told us after the first night they hadn't expected that he would pull through. When he went to theatre for the, first lot of amputations, we'd signed for them to do one kn[ee], one above the knee and one below, but actually the surgeon was brilliant and she managed to save both his knees and so… And that has made a difference to his mobility and things hasn't it?

WILL: Yeah.

HILARY: It yeah, today he's not wearing legs but he does wear legs and he is quite mobile on them for short amounts of time and...short / amounts of time.

WILL: Short amount of time? Well, that's rude.

HILARY: Well, yeah that's not fair I suppose in that you would wear them all day. [WILL: Yes I would.] Yeah, you'd wear them all day wouldn't you? Sorry that's wrong.

Laughs.

I stand corrected.

WILL: Yes, you do.

HILARY: He also has some running blades, have you seen Piscorius? I find it completely frightening to watch if I'm honest. Er, not the normal legs erm, we totally adjusted to that, cos he's developed good balance, although he would still fall over sometimes, wouldn't you? [WILL: I would not!] And then I, and then I would worry cos he swears

WILL intake of breath – shocked

...that's the worst of it. *(Laughs.)* You know on the, on the leaves outside when it's really slippy and [WILL: Oh yeah, that is a problem, yeah.] er, it slips and then he, he swears but [WILL: I don't know about...] the blades, I find the... [WILL: But it is very, very fun!] ...my heart's in my mouth for the blades, because if you do fall *(WILL laughs.)* and of course you're going fast, of course it's much worse.

Laughs.

WILL: Erm, yeah well of course my main goal is to be a swimmer and compete in the Paralympic Games, but before that I want to go to university and do English. I don't know, sort of, whether language or reading it or just English erm, and then erm, do swimming, of course, and then after that [cos you have to retire quite early] erm, just become a journalist. Like a sports journalist and then retire. So, I'm hoping to walk it. Just to walk it, just on my normal legs rather than my running blades just cos I wouldn't trust myself, no to stop or fall, yeah. Or if I find a bin to stop myself.

HILARY: You'll have to run off down somebody's back lane.

WILL and HILARY laugh.

WILL: Daunting.

HILARY: Very special.

WILL: It'll be a very good moment.

SLIDE PROJECTED.

Slide text 'Will carried the Olympic Torch along the banks of the river Tyne June 2012.'

HILARY: Yeah.

SCENE 10

ANNE: [When I arrived in London] This one time I was in London, I just sort of said to myself, 'I could die here and nobody would even know that Anne has died,' but when I was, when I was up North, I think first day, I was, second day, I was already homesick because we went into town and I was so disappointed not to see a black person. And I think it was about the third time, when we went into town, that I saw a black person, yeh, in Newcastle and I was, I just thought they were from Kenya and I was like, 'No maybe I know them or they know me?' And Norman was like, 'No Anne, no, no.'

NORMAN: I've always loved the Angel, I don't know why? But I just love The Angel of the North and I took her across to see it, you know because she's religious and I said well it's called The Angel of the North. 'Why's it called that?' 'Well, come on, we'll see it.' And it was bloody freezing, I mean it was really, this was April as well, bloody freezing. And I said to her, I said, 'You know how we said we would wait until we got married?' She said, 'Yes.' I said, 'I don't want to wait.' I said, 'Do you fancy getting married?' She said 'Yeh, alright.' So I kind of proposed to her under The Angel of the North and then we got married in May. In err, The Civic Centre, in Newcastle, which was a, a fantastic occasion.

ANNE: And then before I knew it I was, I got very ill and I remember I said to Norman, I said, 'Norm, I think I've got malaria.'

NORMAN: Me sister said, I said, 'She's being sick all the time, man, and smells just set her off and she's sick.' She said, 'She's pregnant.' I said, 'What?' I said, 'No, she can't be pregnant.'

ANNE: No, [NORMAN: You'd been told when you were a young woman hadn't ya?] When I was a young woman because of polio and I remember according to the doctors I wasn't able to have, you know, I wasn't able to have kids…

NORMAN: [So] she got pregnant straight away. So we got married and Tim was…came along. That was the end of all the plans of going back to Kenya and everything. And he'll be busting through the door any minute.

ANNE: The doctor said, 'I need you to use a wheelchair to be safe,' coz I was constantly falling over, being on callipers and crutches and so they gave me a day chair and I had Timothy and put on weight as I didn't like being big because I'd been, I was quite small, isn't it? I was very small. And suddenly I'm sort of big and chubby and I didn't like it. So I said to Norman, 'Oh Norman, I need to lose some weight.'

And I went to the gym [in the wheelchair] and one of the running trainers saw me and said, 'You, you could be a very good athlete,' you know. 'There's something called wheelchair racing and you can do that and blah, blah, blah, blah.'

So this one time I'm sitting, you know, sitting in my house, this is 2002 and just going through the channels and I see these amazing women, you know, in their racing chairs, competing. And when Norman came home I said, 'I know exactly what wheelchair racing is and that's what I want to do'. And before I knew it, the running club got me my first chair, my first racing chair, yeh? And I started training and after one year I'd qualified to go to the Paralympic Games. This is 2004 in Athens. Erm, and I went to Athens, coz this time I was still Kenya, I represented Kenya, you know, and…oh, it was, it was magical, oh, it was fantastic! Just the atmosphere and to be on the start line and, you know, when you hear your name being called it's, it's, it's amazing! It's a feeling that you just can't, you just can't explain, you know. I was the first East African person to do wheelchair racing at a high level and I was like, 'Oh my goodness!' You know, I shrugged my shoulders as I was like 'I'm not just racing but I am making history here,' you know, it, it was really good. And after that we got people in Africa talking about wheelchair racing, talking about me and wanting the disabled people to be empowered also and suddenly in, after 2004 erm, parents who, who were sort of hiding or neglecting their disabled kids, suddenly they were like, 'Oh if that girl who is in Europe, in the UK, has done so well…' they also wanted their children to do well.

NORMAN: You did the first Paralympic World Cup in 2005.

ANNE: Yeh, and then I've won gold medals for Great Britain, I've won silvers, I've won bronze medals, you know, different things erm so it's…so it's… I look at it as a journey that started from / nowhere, you know?

NORMAN: But the scary thing is as well, your dad, her dad christened her / Anne Olympia.

ANNE: Yeh, Olympia is my middle name.

NORMAN: But it was all through these callipers, honest, you could do weight training just with the callipers, never mind the crutches that were solid steel as well.

ANNE: Disabled women are so encouraged to get into sport now and I'm involved in so many different organisations that I support disabled women to access sport, you know, and they are using this as erm, as something to empower, to empower the disabled women from different areas. Then I remember we came back here and I sort of just enjoyed the sport and in 2006 I became, no in 2004, I won the Kenyan sports personality of the year and that was my first award for, as an athlete, isn't it? And now working towards 2012, so fingers crossed erm, that will be my last one and it would be good if I went out on a high – but we'll see what happens. Because, because it's, it's interesting. Last year Kenya introduced dual-nationality, so I could either run for Kenya or for Great Britain

NORMAN: I wanted her to go for Kenya.

ANNE: But I want to run, I want to race for Great Britain, yeh.

NORMAN: But I want ya to go for Kenya.

ANNE: I think it would be a privilege to race for Great Britain. I've, I've won so many medals for Great Britain and I've won a few medals for Kenya but for the sake of my son, I would like to race for Great Britain.

NORMAN: That's why I want you to be Kenyan because the British athletes right, getting into the, to the eh, Olympic village, it's like, 'You can't.' I'm like, 'Yeh, but it's me wife.' 'Yes, but that's her son.' But the Kenyans manage to pull some strings and… Timmy had this, I had this badge around me neck and it meant we could go to the Executive Suite and have anything we liked to drink.

ANNE: So that's why he wants me to race for Kenya coz he thinks he'll have free food and booze.

NORMAN: Yeh, coz we get free everything.

ANNE: No. That's why I want to race for Great Britain.

Enter ANNE and NORMAN's son TIMMY.

ANNE: Hello, babes. Hi Timmy.

NORMAN: Just doing an interview, Tim.

ANNE: This is recording.

TIMMY: Looks more like a telephone.

ANNE: Looks like a telephone, yeh? Yeh, it's actually recording, it's actually recording what mammy's saying, yeh.

TIMMY exits.

ANNE: I think my mum would have been so proud of me because erm, you know, there's so many things that I've done now and I always say to myself, 'I wish she was here,' you know? I wish she was here because she would probably appreciated me more then, maybe then, you know, you know? Because maybe, when I've gone through all these stages in life, I think my mam would maybe sort have appreciated it more because it would have meant so much to her, yeh…

SCENE 11

Enter ROGER who addresses the audience.

ROGER: I chased a train the other day. I remember I had to, I had to get the train from Guildford to London and I ran from the car park at Guildford station. And I remember thinking, and I got the train, and as I got on the train I thought, 'I don't think many people would have got that train,' and I was knackered and I was like *(Groans.)* but a part of me thought, you don't, you haven't lost it. You forty-five-year-old… you know. But, I have no concept of the speed I used to run at. None at all. It's…completely a different world of speed. It's not running down the high street to catch a train. It really isn't.

SLIDE PROJECTED.

Slide text 'Stephen Miller. Club Thrower. Gold Medal Atlanta 1996, Gold Medal Sydney 2000, Gold Medal Athens 2004, Silver Medal Beijing 2008. Competing London 2012...'

STEPHEN: ...it ended up working out OK because I ended up winning the club at Athens, and that made it three gold medals in a row...even Stephen Redgrave won bronze on his first one... The only reason that...the only reason that I haven't had the operation to have a new hip, is because I want to compete in London because it's in London, the Olympics and Paralympics...it's a once in a lifetime...

Enter RICHARD COBBING and NICK BEIGHTON.

RICHARD: I wasn't badly behaved, I just had a lot of energy I used to get up very early in the morning... and I, I was all go all day and I never used to sleep very much, but I did have this kind of hyperactivity problem and they'd spoken to their GP and he mentioned that...the...it was a, obviously it was a known condition amongst kids and it was, it was causing them problems.

And in 1972...my dad saw the, the World Trampoline Championships, err, taking place on television, in black and white, Trampolining was quite a new-fangled sort of thing in '72, it had come from The States. And my dad saw this, a clip of this on television, and he went 'That looks like it takes a lot of energy'...and that was...and he said 'Right, that's what we're gonna have to get Richard to do. We'll get him on the trampoline, because if that doesn't burn up energy, then I dunno what will' y'know.'

So there were trampolines around but it was only really accessible to kids who were sort of between, y'know eleven and eighteen-years-old. And I was, y'know, four-and-a-half, almost five-years-old. Erm, so he looked around for a way, he was a plumber, my Dad, he was a plumber in, in Newcastle. So he decided to go out and try and build a trampoline, err, out of materials that were available to him through work: steel pipe, err, and tarpaulin, and stuff like this, and bungee cord…bought some tarpaulin from a trucking, err, from a hauliers, some bungee cord, and made a trampoline. And that was my, I think that was my birthday present for my fifth birthday.

NICK B: I won't, I won't say the, the spare child at the end but I always felt like I had to try and keep up with everyone and always be really competitive so erm, I was pretty hyperactive as a kid actually I was, I'd just run around I was pretty accident prone as well, so I'd run around and trip over everything that I possibly could and break and sprain and cut everything that I could, and jump off walls and fall off cliffs.

So yeah I, I did sport from a, from the earliest of ages so, but you know cross country and athletics and football from, you know, five, six onwards erm, then as I got older, played rugby erm, quite competitively for seven or eight years erm, and mostly rock climbing, tennis and orienteering and all that, you know, sprinting, long jump and endurance running and high jump for a while, shot-put, discus…

RICHARD: And I think as a sort of young, lad, when I was about seven, eight, nine, ten-years-old my motivation for the sport was simply because it was a good time, / it was good fun…

NICK B: …indoor climbing, outdoor climbing, bouldering, soldering, erm skiing, snowboarding. Anything really.

RICHARD: I'd started doing a few competitions then, so there was this sort of sense, even as a youngster, of being able to sort of, have a goal, work towards it, achieve it and then, when you are, when, when you win the medal, it does feel good, y'know.

NICK B: Yeah, but I got really buzz from it, cos I, I love using my body, I see my body as a tool to achieve what I want to err, so it meant I was probably quite brutal to it sometimes, you know. I put it through things that a body shouldn't go through or, you know, I broke it and damaged it a lot in the course of doing what I really love doing.

RICHARD: And, yeah, I mean there's, y'know, winning a sporting competition is a great, it, it's a great feeling, y'know. It's, it's a great feeling whatever you do, whatever sport you do. The, the sense that your…hard work has paid off with you standing on top of a podium…

NICK B: …er, er, I've fractured my skull a couple of times, erm, broken my nose a few times, erm, broken my jaw, perforated ear drums, erm, collar bone, dislocated collar bone…

RICHARD: And that…it's a feeling that you often want more of as well. One you…once you've tasted a bit of success, that can, that in itself drives you on, cause you wanna have that feeling again.

NICK B: …erm, broken wrist, dislocated thumbs, broken fingers, erm, broken ribs, erm, err, like puncturing in my legs and broken ankles er, ripped tendons in my groin, er, broken toes, broken feet…erm, just wear and tear basically. So my mum was forever scraping me up and putting me back together again and sending me off, so… I used to kind of just throw myself at brick walls and just bounce off and laugh and do it again.

RICHARD: First time on an aeroplane, err, and that, that was exciting, that opened up a whole new world of, err, of, of…amazement to me really, y'know the fact that, y'know, this big wide world out there…and, y'know, particularly a young kid coming from the North East of England, you… And it just kind of, I think it set me on a track that I'm still on now…of…sort of existential kind of discovery…

NICK B: I probably wanted to be erm, be an adventurer. I know that's not a job description but I, you know, I, I read books by Ranulph Fiennes and I've like all the mountaineering books. I wanted to see the world, I wanted to do things.

RICHARD: I've learnt to do a bit of Diving as well, competed in Diving…had learned to do a bit of Floor Gymnastics and Tumbling as well, y'know, using these skills that I'd learnt in Trampolining, and wanted to sort of try and put them to good use, and I thought, well I'm gonna sort of forge a career here as a stunt man. So…so I spent, like, time jumping off an eighty-five-foot ladder, err, into a dolphin pool out in, err, in an amusement park in The States in '88.

NICK B: …er, it was part of my pre deployment training, so what they do erm, is, when you know you're going to Afghanistan, you do a certain er, certain amount of training, so we, went out to Kenya, just inland from Nairobi.

RICHARD: It was five shows a day, five forty-five minute shows a day, and, it, yeah, I, I…and including once off the top of the ladder. Which was eighty-five foot, y'know. It's about nine stories up, y'know…

NICK B: …foot patrol err, didn't have any vehicles we were, we were light roll which meant was all carry your kit and on your feet – old school so…so yeah and so we were, we were walking to the, the base it was 800 hundred metres away err, the, the other patrol base…

RICHARD: Well, you have to climb, err, it's, it's the end, it's the end of a show, there's been a forty-five-minute show, there's a, there's an auditorium full of people there, and, the shows been building up with the fact someone's gonna go off the top, and it's your turn, y'know. You're gonna do it. But what you do is, you come out as the audience are waiting there and the, the worst thing about it is, there's this music that's playing in the background, it's part of a

show, so y'know, there's this ver…there's this real doom
laden music *(Laughing.)* playing in the background,
that, err, that makes, what is already a very, err, scary
experience, err, ten times worse, y'know, you've got this
blaring away and, err, it's really…the storm clouds are
gathering as you're climbing up the…as you're climbing up
this ladder…

NICK B: We were about forty metres away from the…from the
front entrance so literally the…the patrol base was here.
We walk along the side of it and we had to come round the
end and in the front end. So we'd walked around the side
of it, we were just coming round the compounds, which
sort of stood out from the front entrance…

RICHARD: …you go up to the, ten metre platform, that's the
top height at Olympic level, it's err, there's a platform
there. And then you go on to the narrow ladder which
is just six inches wide, and you up, there's a sixty-foot-
perch, so there's no… *(Laughing.)* there's nowhere to stand,
y'know, you've just got this little… that's why it's called
a perch, y'know. And then you, you make your way up,
err, to eighty-five feet. You stand on the, very top of this
ladder, it looks like a television mast, is what it sort of looks
like, this thing, and, erm, you turn round, and you look
down and it…everything's got quite small all of a sudden.
Y'know, there's these little faces all looking straight up in
the air at you, y'know, and your heart's going ten to the
dozen and you look down and you go 'God this is really…
I know that I'd better get this right cause it's really gonna
hurt.'

NICK B: It was quite a narrow track with a big wall on one side
and a…an irrigation ditch on the other, erm, so the, the
point man, the platoon sergeant was leading the patrol, two
other guys and then me err, and they all walked past it…

RICHARD: …from even thirty feet you can kill yourself, from
thirty feet, it's possible to kill yourself with the impact on
the water, so from eighty-five feet you have to get things

right. You have to get the…the angle / of, err, of entry in to the water, right, y'know…

NICK B: I trod on it erm so it was a, a home-made bomb essentially erm, fertilizer and a car battery or motor bike battery and some wires and a det…a detonator and two switches. So when you stand on it, it just *(Claps.)* completes the circuit and that goes bang, so…erm, just luck.

RICHARD: … you know you're gonna go, so in a way, that… once that decision's been made that you're going, it's not quite as scary then. You run through what you're gonna do in your head a couple of times, you get ready and you go 'Okay, c'mon let's get this together, let's do it okay. I know what I'm gonna do, concentrate, concentrate, concentrate.' and then just in your head, y'know, you go 'Okay ready… set…dive,' and you just pop off the top of that…

NICK B: …so I it sounds bizarre but in the instant that I trod on it I, I knew what had happened. Literally the split second, the instant as it…as it was happening… I knew what was happening and there was, a real…a frightening sense of…of clar…a frightening sense of clarity and understanding of what this meant for my life. I know that sounds like far-fetched but it's true, like I knew that life was changed forever in that instant and even in the…the millisecond that…that the split second that I was in the centre of this explosion, I knew what it meant.

RICHARD: …you start accelerating *(Laughing.)* what you notice is how quickly you accelerate, and before you know it the wind is rushing past you, and you realise that you're travelling at pretty, y'know, you're going pretty fast. I think you hit the water at about fifty-five or sixty miles-an-hour. So you're sort of going from nought to sixty in…less than three seconds, y'know…

NICK B: Erm, like I still remember that vividly and, you know, I still find myself slipping back to it sometimes and er, it's not so much imagery as a feeling as a…of er…of…feeling of raw power and energy and something being so wildly out of my control, it was just, phenomenal. Really you know, phenomenal. I remember screaming, and I don't know whether I was really screaming or whether it was something inside just going, phrr, why? You know it's a… it's hard to imagine being on top of ten kilos of explosives and standing on it and being in the centre of such a… primeval force and then being thrown through the air an just landing…and the shock and the just, almost the horror, of what's just happened and going through that, it feels quite abstract really, it's quite a strange, strange experience to have really, to relive, you know?

RICHARD: …it's err, just err, understanding where your body is, in space, err, whether you're upside down, or the right way up, or whether you've got another ninety degrees to go before you get your feet underneath you, or whatever it happens to be. And you're using whatever information you can get. The way the wind's blowing against your face, or what you can see, or whether you feel like you're going up, or you feel like you're going down.

NICK B: Ah yeah, I knew what had happened. Yeah I knew my legs were gone. I could tell erm, I knew what damage I…the… I looked but I didn't really look. I didn't feel like I needed to look at my legs to know they were gone.

RICHARD: And I'd spent my whole life jumping off stuff you know and going up and down, upside down and twisting and jumping and flying through the air…

SLIDE PROJECTED

Slide text 'Richard Cobbing. Freestyle skier. Silver medallist world championships. 10th Winter Olympic Games Lillehammer 1994.'

RICHARD: …which is brilliant and exciting but there came a point in life where I was starting to think to myself of like I really need to start forging some kind of career here…

NICK B: It's not a…there's not a point when you decide, right I need to decide what I'm going to do with my life. It's… it's a real, gradual process and humans are amazing at adapting to circumstances, and so, early on, you know, literally the triumph was sitting up in bed or just feeding myself or drinking or being able to lift my arm above, above, you know, three inches and, and you achieve those things, you know. I was very driven as a...as a patient, very driven to push myself and again, you know, I made myself ill on a couple of occasions pushing myself so hard to improve so quickly. But that's how I dealt with it because that's what I'd always done. So I started learning to row in the summer just at Guildford Rowing Club erm, and then GB rowing had a trial in September... Yeah, it's, it's been exciting, you know, cos we've got an amazing opportunity to...to go and compete in London...

SLIDE PROJECTED.

Slide text 'Richard Cobbing. Publican. The Betsey Trotwood, Clerkenwell, London.'

RICHARD: So here we are now at the Betsey Trotwood [pub], been here for four and a half years, y'know we're about real ale and err, we got some nice wines and some nice malt whiskies...

[We've got] another little one Dexter who err, y'know, he err, climbs the walls, Dexter y'know, and he wakes up at five o'clock every morning, y'know, and I'm starting to, I'm starting to sort of, some of these stories that I've heard about me at that age, from my parents are kind of starting to come true now. Yeah, they're allowed to bounce on the bed yeah, yeah, they are allowed to bounce on the bed could, who knows where that's gonna lead, but yes.

SLIDE PROJECTED.

Slide text 'Nick Beighton. Rower, Mixed Pairs. Qualified Paralympic Games 2012.'

NICK B: You know yes I'd love to win a medal and, is that realistic? I don't know, but if I'm going to line up on the start line in front of fifteen thousand fans in Britain in the

Paralympics and have the opportunity to go for a medal is, is that enough? Maybe it is, I dunno.

SCENE 12

CHARMIAN is raised up as if on a diving board.

CHARMIAN: I regret that I gave up diving as soon as I did. I should've gone to Rome, in 1960. I should've done. Erm, cos when Spider Webb came up to Durham and err, he said he'd come back again – and he didn't come back – and err, I started learning a new dive with him and he said how easy it was to teach me a new dive. Erm, and he didn't come back and I thought, that's it, you know, so I didn't continue diving. I regret not going to Rome.

I'm cold, I'm shivering. John, I trust Spider, I trust him and I know he will tell me when to open out and I know I will see the water, I trust him. And I'm climbing up the steps, you don't really think of anything more except each step, one step at a time and then across the five metre and up the next lot of steps. I was dry. I didn't even get wet as I usually do before I went up there. I go to the end of the board [ten metres board] and look down, and I'd see a lot of light coloured water. I turn around and shuffle my heels over the edge and put my arms up. I'd step back onto the board and I'd go through [in my mind] mental rehearsal. Start with my hands up. Jump and get my hips up and curl up and then listen to the…for the sound…and open. So I go back to the end of the board, put my heels over the edge and stand with my toes on the board. Arms up, and into the dive. I hit the water, went down to the bottom came up relieved and everybody was clapping. I hadn't thought. I hadn't realised that everybody was dead silent whilst I went up to do this dive. They had obviously seen me, and my hands are sweating now, just reliving it, yes… so…

SCENE 13

The text is linked by a strong athletic physical sequence evoking the sports depicted. Music swells in and out to emphasise the movement and link the extracts of text.

ROGER: 'Cause people learn from stories. So someone can talk, you know…but it's much better when the examples in the room. And also, it helps that that example is well known and has a few medals and talks about something in the room that no one else will know about. So, we always like to listen to things that we can't do. So, when I stand up in front of people…and it's entertaining, get the medals out, show the races, brilliant.

Music plays.

So the Olympic final is…and you have a destiny, a sort of pre-sense of destiny, you know, you've visualised it so many times but you have to deliver it.

VIV: At the moment the focus is London. Yes. It dominates everything. Even to the point where I don't go and do physio on my legs at the moment. I do a little bit but not enough. And I'm slightly worried that my legs are starting to deteriorate a bit.

ROGER: And it's…it's, you know, you stand there, you wait for the gun, it's…

KAT: I have like, like, a picture in my head, like, of how I want my house to be like, and like, I would have like friends round for tea all the time and I dunno, like, at some point having a family like…

Music swells.

ROGER: You do your warm-up which is the same warm-up you've always done – the same music in your ears in the same way. I was just in my own head. I was there.

ALI: But I thought right, you can't, you can't you know s… you know, you can't give up. You know, you know you're capable… I have to make, I have to imagine that this is the ceiling trying to cave in and I have to push it away. I had to, you know, push the ceiling away from collapsing the ceiling, or I'll die.

Music swells – movement sequence.

ROGER: … In the zone. You walk onto the track, you walk. Eighty-five thousand people but you're just internalising it. You, the moment. You let it out and you go, 'Oh it's the Olympic final, Christ'. You're just…self-dialogue, just keeping it to yourself, you're just there you know, staying calm. You're not thinking about, 'This is the Olympic final. What happens if I mess it up?' I remember it. I remember every bit of it. I remember I was in lane three, Michael Johnson was in lane four. Dunno who was in lane, in all the other lanes. I just know I was in my lane. It didn't matter. You know, you go down to your marks, set. The gun goes…

Music swells – movement sequence.

…you get out as hard as you can. Good start. It's a rhythm that you get into very quickly and you hold that down the back straight. You then maintain it to the…from 200 to 300… And I always knew that if I came out with a 100m to go…and…and if no one was ahead of me, then no one was going to catch me. Now, Michael Johnson was a long way ahead but I knew, I knew that would happen. Well, I wasn't aware of him but I knew… I wasn't aware of him at all but… I could hear my breath. I could hear my head. I could hear my voice *(Makes panting noise.)* and all I could hear was me talking to myself saying, 'High-hips, keep your hips up…don't…keep the shoulders down. Come on, come on, push, push, push, push…'

Music swells – movement sequence.

ANNE: …it's like I couldn't hear people shouting anymore. It was like everything was slow motion, you know, and all I wanted was just to get to the finish line…

ROGER: '…come on, push, push, push, push,' and then the last fifty metres you're just pushing and then you cross through the line and it's relief 'cause it's over, and you've done it. And your life will never be the same again.

ANNE: And everybody was, everybody was so surprised I was like, 'Oh!' You know? I went to get my medal in rain and that medal means so much to me.

ROGER: The medal is the medal. It's not defined by a time and that's it.

I was thirty and I made Michael Johnson cry. He stood up on the Olympic rostrum next to me and just as you turned to hear the national anthem I said to him, 'Michael, this is what it's all about. The prize. Savour this moment 'cause this is what it's all about. And he looked down at me and he broke down. … And I was complete there 'cause I was standing there thinking, 'I've done it…this is… I could…' 'Cause I'd fulfilled my potential 'cause I wasn't going to beat this guy. Yeah, so I came second and that was how it should be.

ANN WAFULA sings as slides roll, communicating the fate of our cast of characters in the Olympic and Paralympic Games 2012.

ANN: Ee Mungu nguvu yetu

    Ilete baraka kwetu

    Haki iwe ngao na mlinzi

    Natukae na udugu

    Amani na uhuru

    Raha tupate na ustawi.

    Amkeni ndugu zetu

    Tufanye sote bidii

    Nasi tujitoe kwa nguvu

    Nchi yetu ya

    Kenya tunayoipenda

    Tuwe tayari kuilinda.

End.

WWW.OBERONBOOKS.COM

Follow us on www.twitter.com/@oberonbooks
& www.facebook.com/oberonbook

www.ingramcontent.com/pod-product-compliance
Ingram Content Group UK Ltd.
Pitfield, Milton Keynes, MK11 3LW, UK
UKHW020727280225
455688UK00012B/538